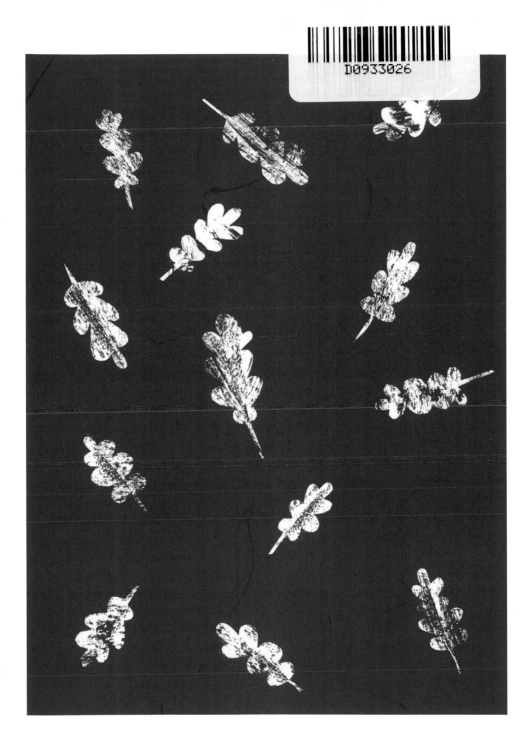

THALIAD

ISBN 978-0-9866909-3-8

Cover and interior artwork by Clive Hicks-Jenkins
Edited and designed by Elizabeth Adams

First Edition

©2012 Marly Youmans

Published by Phoenicia Publishing, Montreal
www.phoeniciapublishing.com

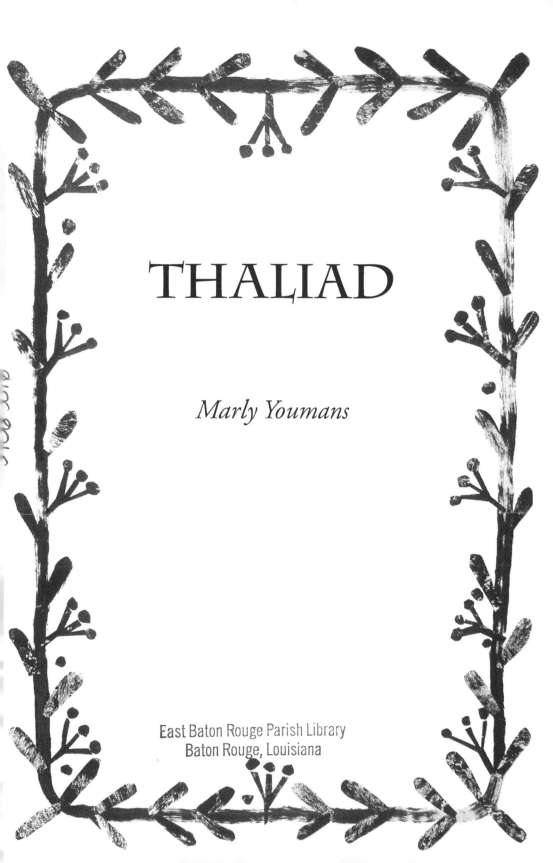

THALIAD

Marly Youmans

ACKNOWLEDGMENTS

Portions of *Thaliad* have appeared in *Mezzo Cammin* and the *Journaling the Apocalypse* issue of *qarrtsiluni*.

THALIAD

 *To John Wilson and Paul Digby*

I. Luring the Starlit Muse

YEAR 67 AFTER THE FIRE

*Emma declares what she knows about the time before the fire
and calls on a starlit muse, the only love she will ever have,
to tell the hero's saga of The House of Thalia and Thorn.*

It was the age beyond the ragged time
When all that matters grew disorderly—
When artworks changed, expressive, narcissist,
And then at last became just tedious,
A beetle rattling in a paper cup,
Incessant static loop of nothingness,
When poems sprang and shattered into shards,
And then became as dull as newsprint torn
And rearranged in boredom by a child
Leaning on a window seat in the rain.
Then beauty was abolished by the state
And colleges of learning stultified,
Hewing to a single strand of groupthink.
It was a time bewitched, when devils ruled,
When ancient ice fields melted, forests burned,
When sea tossed up its opal glitterings
Of unknown fish and dragons of the deep,

When giant moth and demon rust consumed,
And every day meant more and more to buy.
Some people here and there lived otherwise,
But no one asked them for any wisdom,
And no one looked to their authority,
For none they had, nor were they like to have
The same—no one expects the end of things
To come today, although it must some day,
And so no one expected the great flares
That kissed the world with bright apocalypse.
And now no one recalls that day of fire,
For all are dead who might have seen the thing:
Only a few survived the scathing hour.

I was not one of those—I was not born
To evil days and came belatedly
To this, a world transformed—thanks be to she
Who floats on spirit wings above the lake,
Turning and returning on her pinions,
Sweeping and calling in the summer's light
Or in the shining clang of winter ice.
So let me have the blessing of that bird
When story's word comes streaming from my mouth,
Igniting joy around the evening fire
Of driftwood limbs and pinecones on the shore.

And let me, daughter of the royal house
That is the only household in this place,
Take for my muse the boy seen inwardly,
Glimmering along the spits of flotsam.
How he evades the swaddling bands of time!
I scoop my hand and let world's history
Sift through my fingers, pottery and glass
From those who lived and died three hundred years
Before the blast… The boy is beautiful,

And starlight seethes beneath transparent skin
To light his veins until they're silvery,
A tree of magic wands that curl and pulse
Toward the chamber of the muse's heart.
Look on me kindly, boy who glows like moon
And treads the sand and waves of Glimmerglass.
Inspire me in the ways of ink and pen
And help me to make from these paper leaves
A book to tell and bind the hardest times
That ever were in all of history,
To make a story worthy of the one
Who lived past fire to wield the spear and sword
As if time tumbled up the hourglass,
Who by adventure saved her own from death
Or else allowed us to be born in peace.
Ah muse, be kind and loving now to me.
I went out years ago to take your hand,
Searching for a man as is the custom
Of women when our blood begins to seep
And cry out to create a newborn child,
But found that you were never in the flesh,
Seemingly immortal in your beauty—
And so I am now married to the quill,
Always watching for your dreamy footsteps
No heir shall come to me, nor childbed death,
Nor life made plentiful with girl and boy,
Nor age beside a husband and the hearth:
Whoever and whatever you may be,
Shine constantly on me with your strange grace
That I might tell the story of one who
Was ordinary as a stone or stem
Until the fire came by and called her name.

II. The Angel by the Door

OF YEAR I, THE FIRE AND AFTER

*Emma recounts what family has told of the fire and stone-fall
and how Thalia took hold to lead her friends into the sunlight.*

I was not born and cannot say the truth
Save in the sparse outlines of fairy-tale,
A skeleton once fleshed in moving life,
Just as the tales were passed to me from those
Who bore the day—those few inside the cave
Who felt the earth uprooted from its place,
Who saw the stones unhinged and slammed to ground,
The mothers and the teachers crushed by rock
That kept the living from a quick return.
But Thalia, the youngest to survive,
Declared an angel burned beside the door,
A figure made of fire that stabbed its shafts
Of light inside the darkness of the cave.
I have no wish to doubt that witnessed sight,

Although she was so young; the others who
Saw that strangeness died before my birth-time.
In those days was a ceremony named
The *field trip,* questing to a noted spot—
Why that place was picked is now forgotten.
Perhaps the cave's initiation ring
Was famous, or perhaps rhinoceros
And mammoth, bison, lion, hyena,
And horse were daubed in red and black on walls
As I have found in pictures from a book
Of lands across the sea that none of us
Have ever seen, and none likely to see.
Calamity had burst around the group—
With shrieks the children tried to rouse the ones
Already mashed and dead, and some began
To tug at legs or arms turning to wax.
Fear-slayer Thalia called to the rest
To calm themselves, and also gathered up
The flashlights and the precious sacks of food,
Arranging them in piles along the floor.
The insects and the bats were left unstirred
By devastation, hanging upside down
To sleep or watch the children wail and weep,
All but Thalia, guardian of those
Remaining in the world of stirring life.
Some few who lay within the borderlands
Of life and death were murmuring a while,
But no help came, and so they bled and died.

Their dead lay strewn and broken under stones,
And yet the children managed to forget
A while, although each pebble's slide and drop
Reminded one or more of tragedy—
And yet they played an hour of flashlight tag
Inside the tomb, as if at home and safe.

I wonder whether that is something good,
To let the terrible dissolve in play,
Or whether it is just a mockery,
And says how little human beings feel.
Must every good be brought to light by work,
And nothing pure be native to our selves?
Yet little Thalia gives hope to me
That better traits belong to humankind
Than history recounts… The dead meant more
For the living, more batteries and food.
She made them play at soldiers, guard the sacks
And hoard the waning, precious glow of lights.
Slowly they worked loose stone out of the mound
That choked the archway leading to the air.
The smallest, she became the one to first
See trees again, and worm her way through rocks
And call excitedly that she could glimpse
A steeple pointing to the darkened sky.
She led the hungry children down the path,
And when no cars appeared along the road,
She marched them down the highway's center line.
Just seven boys and girls survived that hour.

In later years, she never would describe
Her feelings, finding streets emptied of life,
Where shadows of a tree, a woman's hand,
The reaching arm of a young child were burned
Onto sidewalks and walls—not one of them
Found family at home, unless they were
Corpses, and the rest evaporated
As if they'd flown to some bad fairyland.
How long the children lingered in the place,
I do not know, but Thalia became
The one who urged them through the town to search,
Who had them raid a shop that stank of meat

And threw a picnic underneath a tree,
Who hijacked grocery carts to gather food,
Who kept them close, who made them hide and seek
On commons ground that once had been alive
With daily to and fro but now was gloom—
And then she told them that the act was done,
How they'd no time to wail below the lour
Of skies that wept in ash and turned the day
To twilight, an uneasy, changeless dusk.
If we stay here, then we will die, she said,
As everyone we ever loved has died.
The brute pronouncement shocked them clean of tears,
At least a little space, and they obeyed
Her orders, scoured the streets for cars with keys—
In a merchant's showroom, the doors flung wide,
They found a van already fueled and piled
Inside, the seven leaping on the seats
Or jolting to the floor with shrill, mad cries.
Then Thalia announced, *We'll drive in turns*
Because it can't—can it?—be all that hard.
They whooped when walls swung near and shouted praise
As she stamped the pedal; they shot from lanes
Of stickered cars and lurched onto the road,
Swinging, wavering: she called for them to *hush.*
The compass on the mirror edged toward North.
Until we find a place where skies aren't grayed
And densed with clouds, she murmured to herself,
Her hands gone moist, the steering wheel tight-clutched,
Her leg extended till the foot could shove
Down on the pedal—shimmying, the car
Began to surge until the children screamed,
The wine of brave adventure in their blood.

III. Seven Against the World

Year 1

*The seven are introduced and given a genealogy
by Emma, bard of tales to the right-royal House of Thaliad*

These were the ones who lived beyond the cave,
And now in after-times are hailed by me,
Chosen by Thalia to be the bard
Of history and chant beside the fire,
Confess our tale and warn the clave of pride
That breaks in atoms all the flowery world.
Foremost of those I would now praise is she,
Thalia, the leader, little mama,
Renewer of the company of souls
That elsewise might have languished, sickened, died,
Their very cells corrupted by the fire,
A seething bane, invisible in blight
If what the libraries reveal is truth.
Her mother was Althea, physician,

Famous for her healing gifts and knowledge,
Busy and swift, beloved of Thalia.
Her father was unknown, donor of seed,
Impregnator without shape, a formless
Father of the mind who though a mortal
Receives immortal honors from our kind.
Next was Samuel, clever with his hands,
Not thoughtful or a one for words but brave
And kind when anyone was needing help.
His mother was a clerk, a woman known
As one who liked to laugh, tell jokes, and sing
In karaoke bars—merry places
Now snuffed in dark and lost to humankind
So that we hardly know to speak the word
That meant to croon with music from a box.
His father was an officer of law,
A master of the gun and beating stick,
Who chased his enemies and locked them fast
Until the hour came to set them free,
Alhough how they knew is past our knowing.
Sophrasia known as Fay, adroit with routes,
Played the navigator on their travels.
She had a gift for prying out their needs
And always managed to discover maps
In barren stations, stores, or tourist stops,
Reading roads to chart a clear-cut journey.
Her father, Jeremiah, was a priest
In Holy Church of the Redempted Life,
A singer and a twister of sweet words,
A hyperbolic master of alarm
And fine resolves, a rouser of the slug
And indolent, the sinner, liar, thief.
Maria was her mother, elegant
But prone to fatal pride, her husband claimed—
Sophrasia disagreed and was the chief

Of all Maria's loves, or so she vowed.
That mother voice could shake the roof-beams free
Of dust and spiderwebs, could float and move
A mighty vault of arches flushed with light.
The strongest child was Randolph, nicknamed "Ran,"
His brawn so needful, first within the cave
But vital many times along the road.
His parents owned a store of handy things
Like hammers, boards, and shingles for a roof,
The sort of stockpile people long to find
When towns are rank with weeds and walls decay,
And world seems cankered, slumping into death.
His mother, Mary-Anna, kept the books,
His father, also Randolph, minded shop,
The two of them remarkable for joy,
Contentment, and an easy-going life.
The twins were Alexandra and Elaine,
Inseparable, identical as nails
Made by machine and shot inside a box
Back in the days of shining factories.
They were the only blood-linked family
Among the Thalians who journeyed far
From shade of stacked-high thunderheads of ash
To find a cloudless, safer place to live,
And often talked of home, their arms entwined,
And parents, Juliet and Tom, who owned
A bed-and-breakfast—one of them shaped wood
And crafted chairs and tables of the burled
And bird-eyed timber those with taste admired,
The other plied a great 8-harness loom
To weave the throws, scarves, and silken shawls
Desired by wealthy people of that day.
The last yet first in many ways was he
Who showed how tubes could siphon gas from cars,
How tanks of fuel nested near farmyard barns—

Gabriel was his name, the one who wept
Too often for the others' peace of mind,
Who muttered names of much-loved dead until
The others called to him to *shut up, now!*
For weren't they all the very same in grief?
The ones he named, Miguel and Carlos, Liz
And Nancy, must have been his family,
But who was who is lost to history.
Perhaps Miguel was father to the boy,
Proud of his intelligence and tender
Manner, worried that he was so loving
And peaceable where other boys were wild,
High-spirited and quick to buck and shout.
And maybe it was Liz who cradled him
When he was sad at some recalled offense
Or playground gibe that jabbed him to the quick,
Who knew his lassitude to be the fount
Of dream and understood how dreaming may
Be portent of a greater life to come.
Now with my pen I pray that it was so!

IV. Gabriel the Weeper

YEAR 1 AFTER THE FIRE

The endless mourning of a boy. A highway, drear or harrowing.
A moment of wild thoughtlessness that sealed the end of innocence.

Beyond the blasting fire, all roads are long;
The children wearied of the way before
The path was hours old, complained or yelled,
And, taking turns, pushed north across state lines.
Some slept and woke to see the landscape changed
From mountains into hills and farmers' fields,
Though seldom did they see a sign of life
Except for deer and red-tailed hawks and birds—
One time a bellowing blockade of cows
Scared the children into shouts or silence,
As was the nature of each one, but Ran
Declared the herd was crying to be milked.
We will need milk, said Thalia, *so sniff*
And find the path to where we're going, cows!

At that remark, the weeping Gabriel
Let out a snort, hiccupped, and laughed out loud:
See those long rows of green, he said to her,
And then those wavy hills? One day I walked
Up there with my father. I'm sure it was
The place. It could have been… It looks the same.
We found a sourwood tree that had been killed
By something, but the leaves still drooped in place,
Though every one had faded into brown.
When we came closer, leaves burst into wings—
The tree was green, the death was butterflies,
Alive and pouring like a waterfall
But upside down from us. His gentle voice
Lingered in her mind, but when she answered,
He had begun to cry and did not hear.
Bespelled by dust, a seeming-endless track
Unreeled before the van, and soot was snow
That fell from blackened wings of butterflies.
Two boys once sprinted from a wood and chased
The car to hurl chunks of concrete and stones
At frightened faces pressed against the glass—
Sophrasia, driving, jammed the pedal down.
Stone-kissed, a window blossomed spiderwebs.
They hated us! Did you see they were burned?
What did they want with us? What would they do
To us? Don't trust—don't stop—don't listen—don't!
They might have killed us or done something worse…
What's worse? I don't know but there might be worse.
There's things teenagers know that we don't know.
But I know everything, there's nothing worse.
And so do I, and I say there is worse.
What's worse? Who says what's worse? What is the worst?
Who cares? Let's always run and not find out.
We ought to have—we ought to have a gun.
You never shot a gun! You'd shoot yourself.
I never would! What I say is just this:

No trusting anybody over twelve.
No trusting anybody. No. No trust.
I wish we didn't have to stop again.
It's time to look for gas, it's almost time.
I want my mother and my father back...
I want them back, I want, I want them back.
And suddenly it seemed adventure was
An overrated thing, and dread humped high
And firm as stone outcroppings on the hills.
I wish that nothing ever happened to me,
Gabriel whispered to the spider's web
That fractured passing pictures of the land,
I wish, I wish, I wish that nothing came
Trampling across the sky to me. To me!

The seven tilting with the world were young,
Remember that—had lived impossibly
Plush lives as in the shining magazines
That linger here and there, with shots of cars
In colors we no longer see on Earth,
Women shrunk and twisted into poses
Impossible to hold yet beautiful,
Painted pouting, more like fairy glamour
Than anything that labors, eats, and dies,
With houses where the rooms are warm and gleam
No matter how it snows, or how the ice
Collects in ropes along the crooked eaves:
World was one way, and then it changed, it changed.
The children squabbled over who would drive
Until nobody wanted any more
To pilot or to ride, and half were sick,
Their soda cans and candy wrappers strewn
Across the floor where Gabriel was tucked
In a fetal curl and weeping steadily.
The world grew dusky, noiseless, and the birds
Dying in flight came pelting from the sky

Till all the air was hushed, and Gabriel
Seemed long and loud though weeping quietly,
And so the children kicked their legs at him
And shouted for him to *shut up, shut up!*
Yet Gabriel kept on with low-toned sobs
As if he meant to hurt no peace of mind
But weep until he'd washed the bitter shard
Of grief from out its mortal housing—heart
That could not change with change, nor summon up
A different rhythm for a different day.
They reached a river's giant flood, a bridge—
One bridge among the many, highway spans
And one black trestle that meant trains once crossed
Though everything was silent as in dreams
Except the children shrieked for Gabriel
To be a mute, a stone, a block, a tree
Or anything that had no voice to speak.
Let's put him down! Let's shove him out and leave!
Yes! Yes! Yes! I can't stand him
Another moment more, this terrible
Crybaby noise. Who couldn't cry—I will
If he does not shut up! Let's put him down!
The van was spraddled sideways in the road,
And children tumbled from the sliding doors,
Accompanied by gay confetti bits
Of bags and wrappers and by tinny sounds
From cans that bounced and reeled across the road.
They dragged him from his lair beside a seat,
They shouted at him that he'd learn a thing
Or two, to not be so unendingly
Unbearable, to weep as all could weep
But did not do. He'd learn a lesson, two
Or three or more; he could cry as he liked
And let nobody hear or care a whit,
Cry to the wilderness of trees and ash
And let the earless creak and saw response.

15

He huddled on the pavement, sunk in tears,
And only jumped up, pleading at the glass
When laughing faces looked from high on him.
I'd like to say that they relented then,
Embraced the boy and let him in to stay,
One cruel lesson roughly taught and learned:
Events went otherwise. They drove away.

They drove away! And left that little boy
Alone with bridges, river, blowing ash,
Immensity. He was eleven, a child
Beloved and seldom left alone in rooms.
The landscape must have wallowed round his head,
Wavering, frightful-strange, making its threats
In symbol language of a mighty sky
That promised death, destruction, reign of fire;
In symbol language of the puissant stream
That had been thicked and porridged by the ash
Yet shoved on journeying to God knows where—
To the sea! A place where he had knelt with pail
And shovel, scooping castles from the sand,
Or floated on the spume, his father near,
Or walked the water's edge to see the life
That bubbled out of holes after a wave.
Perhaps he also thought of one great crash
That grasped and muscled him into the sea,
The briny drink corrosive to his throat
—Current's undertow, the helpless jostling
Said he was nothing cherished by water—
Perhaps recalled the slide of foreign flesh
Against his thigh, the fright of feeling death
Move coldly by (the temperature of waves
No colder) and the waves not frolicsome
As waves could seem when shattered into foam
Around his toes, though sucking toward the drain
As lappings dragged and undermined his feet.

A mile beyond the bridge-end, Thalia
Shrieked riot into order, sued for peace,
Commanded that they turn for Gabriel.
They laughed and mocked but soon agreed and vowed
They'd meant to do no more than stop his tears,
No more than plug the noise, the endless noise,
The wretched soundtrack to a trip that none
Would ever ask for, never dream to wish,
And so they spun the wheel and headed South—
The bridge hove into view, as broad and long
As it had been before: *Not here, not here,*
A little farther, no, I think we've passed
The spot. Look there, I spy his purple shirt.
Three times they drove the distance of the bridge,
But nothing did they see, nothing at all
Of Gabriel the weeper, vanished, gone
As if a messenger had flown to Earth
And snatched him up to ashless paradise.
I pray that it was so! The children paused
And peered in murky waters where some saw
A smudge of purple, flash of hand, but no
One could agree another's sight was true;
They wandered, calling aimlessly his name
But louring clouds ate up the echoed word,
And children soon will tire of any game.
They drove away again. The silence begged
Its questions. Children foraged, slept, and woke
To meet another ashen day. At times
A question begged for silence. Children leave
The past behind and change, but silence stays
As road to inwardness, and questions beg.
All day they did what needed to be done,
Though silence looked in on them now and then,
And after hours of hush and lassitude,
Often one would speak and words seem alien,
Half prophetic and frightening to hear:

And now we are six, murmured Thalia,
When we were one, we'd just begun, when we
Were two, were nearly new, when we were three,
Were hardly us, when we were four, were not
Much more, when we were five, were just alive.
But now we're six, as clever as clever,
So let's be six forever and ever.
And Samuel leaned forward, asked *What's that?*
Nothing, just a poem I changed a bit
To make it fit for us. It's called The End.

v. The Blood of Warriors

YEAR 1 AFTER THE FIRE

Dark stars, uneasy constellations strewn across the children's path,
with Thalia at risk: they armed themselves against all unknown foes.

They grew accustomed to the look of death,
Knew how to edge around a bloated corpse,
Seeing and unseeing, glancing at edge
And not at face or form or anything
That might be moving underneath a shirt—
Becoming scavengers of the lost world,
The raiders of hotel and summer camp,
The ones who tarried by the road to pluck
A farmer's orchard fruits, warm with the sun.
The siphoners, the grocery-store thieves
Who pilfered what seemed edible from stench
Of bloody bins and blue-furred vegetables
And aisles waist-deep in avalanche of stock.
Easily distracted, they made stops
At county fairgrounds, weirdly stilled and hushed,
Or ranged through echo chambers of a mall
And seized whatever crossed the mind—to eat
Or drink or wear, and over days the van

And even rooftop carrier was crammed
With toys to hug, stuffed animals and dolls
That unknown to themselves they really loved
In subterranean and hidden ways
As mother, father, boundless giant toys
Embraced by children who had shown more bent
For a Pied Piper's games, electric pulse
Of bright fantastic worlds or pounding war
On boxes that seemed supernatural.
In those days magic reached its apogee,
And very few had mastery of toys
That held, enchanted, children in their power:
But wizards could not loose themselves from death,
And all that magic drained out of the world.
One day they paused beside museum walls
And stared at bodies tumbled there—in black,
These men who must have died beyond the fire,
Their pooling blood gone glass-glaze slick beside
The muscled arms now freed of weaponry,
A mismatched battery of guns and shields
That days before had skittered from their grasp.
A constellation of spent bullet shells
Enclosed each fierce and geometric stance
As if each longed to be a Hercules,
A Polophylax or Orion, fleet
As hero warriors, guardians of light
Tacked up by stars against macadam sky.
When Thalia bent over one of them,
A hand shot out and clenched her by the throat,
Shaking her slightly till the others screamed.
The rasping voice demanded they fetch drink
And did not let her go—he gulped and choked
On Ran's warm orange *Crush*, then vomited,
His fingers tightening on Thalia's neck.
Their voices were as small and twittering

As birds that chirped for freedom from a cage.
Then Fay, perhaps inspired by memories
Of fluent voices, oratory, word
Of power lifting over lifting faces,
Knelt close to him, and taking Thalia's hand,
Cried out against the fingers on that throat,
For in the broken, new-made name of Christ,
She said, *and by the Holy Spirit's wings*
That swirl around your dying, aching head,
Let go this innocence, let go of her
Who never did a harm to you or yours—
Remember that your soul will stand in hours
Or instants at the haloed throne of God,
Remember that this is the last good deed
That you can ever do, remember life,
The sweetness of the air against your face
That comes like touch of someone dear to you
But dead and gone and never coming back,
Remember how that one would linger near
When you were ill or feeling low and dull.
His hand relaxed and set the trembling child
Free: then he shuddered once or twice and rasped
A syllable—perhaps it was just *life*—
And died, his eyes still fastened onto Fay's.

After shockwaves ebbed, when words of anger
And warding-off were spilled like dice from cups
And each had touched the prints on Thalia's neck,
They wandered through the long museum halls,
Collecting what seemed good to them to own
In their defense—no guns, but morning star
And metal shield, swashbuckling leather rounds
Light on the arm, transparent riot shield,
A curling Turkish dagger, blades of bronze
And tempered steel, katana, knife, and swords

Engraved with prophecy or name and lines
That might have been a blessing or a curse,
Bone-handled rapier and smallsword decked
In tendrils of a flower no one knew,
Axes, hammers, glaives, and ring-mail hauberks.
When Alexandra cut her leg with a blade
Described as Fragnarach, the Irish sword
Famous for its power over breezes,
Lies (those windy mouthfuls of air), or men
And joined by name to Norse lore's Ragnarök
That promises world's end and then rebirth
Through two who live by sipping dew from leaves,
The others bound the slash with Chinese silks
That once had cauled an edge of watered steel.
War gear mixed strangely with their animals,
The pink plush elephant, the cheetah, cats,
Koala, cockatiel, assorted dogs,
And all the furry denizens of Van,
That moving castle, always heading North.

VI. Anointed by the Clave

Year 59 After the Fire

Emma, recalling her anointing by the matriarch's own hand,
affirms that she was named as bard and record keeper by the Clave
and so is worthy to recount the histories of Thalians.

Eleven, I was brought before the Clave
That is the forum of full-grown adults
Because each child of age is charged to learn
One mastery from all that's meaningful
And needed by our tribe—of medicine,
Of roofing or repairing cottages
And buildings, of our waterworks, of wood
That fuels our houses in the wintertime,
Of speaking to the world beyond this world
And catching souls in nets of liturgy,
Of foraging beyond the bounds of home,
Of fighting foes and ravening pack dogs,
And every craft for creeping through this world
Of wilderness and weather, hard to brave
And rule without an understanding mind.
The council met in church, where rainbow light
Expresses hope and promise to the Clave,

Where fire-annealed glass figures stand around
To watch and bless us, and the bird in flight
That is the burning spirit of the Lord
Is caged with lead and crowned in amber glass.
They stayed me at the lych-gate, made me halt
Until the matriarch was on her throne
To ponder with the others what would be
My fate. Then one came walking with a wand
Of gold that crested in the sacred cross
Where profane hours bisect the infinite,
Reminding us that all our agonies
Are no more than an eye-blink in the scheme
Of endlessness, that even God has borne
Fell shiverings as nails were slammed in flesh.
She led me in that haunt of holiness,
Chaotic bulk, obscurity to eyes
Until the altar became visible
In shade, lit solely by the light through glass,
Unearthly flesh made ravishing by sun,
Streaming forth a luminist's enchantment,
Bathing me in a mist of shining motes.
The matriarch looked fearsome in her robes,
A ruler I had never glimpsed before,
Though I had seen her daily all my life.
She raised her arms and charged the Clave to be
A witness to the high anointing hour,
Entrusting me to labor and to serve.
Her thumb that stroked the scented holy oil
In shape of time crossed by eternity
Was rough as if a hand carved out of wood
Had kissed my forehead with its fragrant sap.
This child is now a woman of the Clave.
Long we have called her Emma, bookish girl
Who bends her heart toward poetry and tales,
But now we shall devote her to the word
And deed her to the first of useless things,

The ones that jar the soul but are not drink
Or hoe or medicine or daily bread,
Though some go ill and hungering for them.
Today we name her Emma, Bard of Clave,
Who'll make a record of our passing years,
As if the stone of the philosophers
Were letters, ink and pen, or printing press
To transmute copper coin of hours to gold:
I charge her now to speak of us in words
Translucent to the people, yet aspire
To flower into syllables of joy
And sorrow like the famous bards of old
Who knew their tools and unashamed to sing
Inspired by holy spirit or the muse
Danced on rhythmic feet into the twilight.
And also I enjoin her to become
High Storyteller of the fallen world,
Preserver of the knowledge of the past,
Librarian of Clave, to judge the books
And winnow dross, to forage for the best
In dangerous far regions of the land,
To guide our children in the paths of taste
And learning, for the coming world shall be
Made better than the one that died before—
So save the best of the inheritance
Ancestors passed to us, encourage hope
That we in time can learn to speak as well
As they. Despite the rigor of this life,
I have long loved our little library,
And wish that all my children's children gain
A care for books and culture so we may
Be civilized, upholding right and law,
Embellishing our lives with graciousness.

I tire, remembering the matriarch,
The moments when she taxed me to pursue

Impossibles, the pegasus of art,
The mastery of verse, the library
With all the stored-up wisdom of the world,
And so the trivial floats into mind
As I recall a gown of champagne silk
My mother foraged from a dead girl's house:
How delicate it was, the bodice rich
With seeded pearl, the rest a blossoming
Of cloth in petal on petal, swathed in tulle . . .
For years I have been forager of books
And ventured out with sword and shield and flame
On quests that roving gangs of dogs despise,
A blade and buckler to defend my back,
Exploring libraries now tenanted
By owls, their scholars only ghosts of dust
To make me tremble at a touch of breath
And whirl abruptly in familiar fear,
Half longing for a solid face and form
To then resolve from shadows of a room.
But this is not my tale. All I've declared
Was said to prove that I am rightful bard,
Anointed by the hand of Thalia,
Although I'm not yet worthy of the task
And hardly fit to speak high histories
Of matriarch or seven Thalians,
Orphaned children wandering in blindness,
And how six came to settle on this shore
When world's so wide. The sparkles of a fire
Beside the lapping endlessness of lake
Ascend, and children clamor for accounts
Of journeying and risk and dire mistake,
And so I shape the words in mind: begin.

VII. The Profane Madonna

Year 1 After the Fire

*How an evil came from the sword—and how a strange encounter left
each longing for a mother: to be home and someone's child again.*

Three days they slumbered in a lotus land
Of pleasure, floating in a murky pool
Or roaming in a maze of corridors…
They bounced from one king-size bed to the next
Or lazed in lotus-eater style in suites
Until the twilight sailed them off to dreams
While in each chamber blinded cyclop eyes
Reflected play-tossed, tumbled shapes of sleep.
They left, refreshed, though Alexandra's wound,
Inflamed and angry, made them ransack stores
For bandages and salve, familiar names
Inside the hidden worlds of pharmacies,
Forbidden realms of drugs and mystery,
The mortar and the pestle, snowy garb
Establishing the purity of priests
And priestesses of sacred medicine.
Antibiotics may have saved her life,
Though she was ill and nauseous many days;

They paused to give her tranquil hours to heal,
Camping in the rambling warren of a house
Tucked in a roadside orchard—apple, peach,
And cherry trees in ranks around the home,
A larder laden with preserves and jams,
The kitchen stinking, foul with putrid meat
The children hoisted, lugged across the yard.
Then vultures gathered, fierce, with bald red polls
And gangly wings, and lesser scavengers
Made feints to snatch at shreds of tattered flesh
Until the ground was dabbled dark with blood.
Abandoned cats came slinking through the weeds—
Their energy, compressed and coiling, hugged
The earth or streaked wild-eyed to the tree-tops,
Flew flashing, knocked a raven to the earth…
No clowder of feral cats could dislodge
Feasting vultures, so they snatched and scampered
With dripping gobbet mouthfuls in their jaws.
On the third day, when Alexandra rose
From bed, they had a chance encounter in
The orchard's heart—Elaine, quick-eyed, cried *Hush!*
And drew them backward into orchard trees
To watch the pair of strangers straying past
Their hiding place: a girl of seventeen
Perhaps, a younger boy who seemed to lead
The other as if he had rule of her.
Then Thalia made haste to greet the two,
Speaking quietly with words of welcome.
What is it? cried the girl and clutched at him
Who spread his arms to shelter her from wrong.
Her clothes were stained with blood; she looked around
All querulous and birdlike, tilting her head
As if to catch the slightest threat of sound.
It isn't them, he said, and pressed her close
Until she wept, relieved and unashamed

Of showing gladness—then he raised her hand
And grazed their faces with the fingertips.
I was afraid, I was afraid that you
Were them returned to hurt me once again—
The sun boiled up from earth and was transformed
Into a spinning pillar-cloud of fire,
Not God to lead me through a wilderness
But demonkind that shut me in a jail
And blinded all the world against my sight.
Then scorching devils came, but voiced as men,
And did with me according to their will,
Their scalding will… I felt the seed of flame
Implant inside my womb and when I woke
This child was by my side and cried to see
My hurt, my fear, my wild dishevelment,
And then I knew he was my only son,
Born out of darkness, out of blinding pain,
Transformed from infant into little boy
And given for my comfort in the world
That he should guide me through the shadow land
To paradise where we can live in joy…
So have you seen a peaceful dwelling place
Where we can be a mother and a son
Without the world encroaching on our love?
Then Thalia, with kind persuasive words,
Began to say that they should come along
In faring north to find a better realm,
And all the others joined with her to beg
And say that she could be their mother too.
I have one only, just one child, she said,
This blessing that bloomed forth from blood and pang,
And how I could have more without the pain
And fright—I cannot bear the pain and fright!—
I do not know. You others must belong
To women who are searching for you now,

For I belong to him and him alone,
And God shall find out all the secret crimes
That are a blackened orchard in the heart
Of romping devils who are jeering now
And snap their fingers at the thought of law
And right, whose terror hands are sprinkling blood,
Whose faces simulate the looks of men
But who by feint and covert action mine
And spoil the happy garden of the world.
Now listen! Somewhere devils practice hate
Upon the dazzling body of a girl,
But I will go and chase them with my son
Until their pent-up evil bursts in flame,
A conflagration self-consuming, self-
Annihilating, justice, pillared fire!
She blundered off between the orchard trees;
They would have followed her and begged again,
Except the boy dragged up his shirt to show
A blunt-nosed gun that dug into his thigh
And warned them off. *For we are two alone,*
And she is mine, the only mother left
In all the world, and we want nothing else
But peace, to find a garden place to till
Where vultures cannot come, where peace abides,
And there I'll lead her by the hand to dew
And flowers, show her all the gentleness
That died in fire can be reborn in me.
He swerved away and ran with her through trees
And left the children staring after him,
Enchanted into stillness by surprise.

VIII. The Lake of Prophecy

YEAR I AFTER THE FIRE

*Thalia abandoned maps and followed a wing-shaped patch of blue
to a lake with a tower where bright revelation seared her mind.*

The heavens, ichorous, let down a rain
That seemed as if it could have been the blood
Of dying gods dreamed up in ancient worlds,
The shining fluid, Aphrodite's blood,
The blood of Psyche, muses, maenads, Love,
The blood of Ares, fluent Hermes, Zeus,
A silvery discharge that spattered glass
And clung in pooling drops against the hood
As if to kiss with tears of mercury,
Though those ethereal blood drops soon changed
To drops from ulcers, acrid on the skin…
Then Thalia felt doubt about the path,
Uneasy lest the children should have gone
From South to greater South, and wandered till

They struck the way to Mexico and passed
Along the curling land bridge to the top
Of South America, for darkened day
Seemed doom: they veered to pass catastrophe
Of black, the towering of solid cloud,
Castellate and jagged as if giants
Had reared a gargoyle fortress in the sky.
They swapped the van and fueled beside a farm
Where stalks of corn were seared and overthrown
And vegetables hunched rotten in the leaves.
They moved because to stop seemed death, though none
Matched words to fears that haunted Thalia
And must have roiled them all with secret dread.
She thought of poison in preserving jars,
She thought of radiance that pierced the skin
With acupuncture meaning death to come,
She thought of waterfalls that could not rinse
The taint of evil from their water-drops…
And slept, her head cupped by a leather shield,
Then woke to cries—a wing-blade, purest blue,
That tore apart the battlements of cloud.
Ignoring maps, they seized upon that shape
As omen of some better hope to come,
An arrowhead that meant to point a path
When there appeared no outlet from the blight
Of shadow from tremendous rock-hewn clouds.

Two hundred miles away, the sky restored
Its simple blue and widened till the blade
Became a chalice set between the fogs
Of filth and desolation—Thalia,
Awakened, turned the wheel, while others slept
As children sleep, entirely overthrown,
Their eyelids flickering with mysteries
Of dream, and unfamiliar visages

Seemed masks across each ordinary face.
She felt as if she fared deep in a dream—
The others sprawled like strangers on the seats,
Helpless, distant, dumb to stop her choosing,
And she, unchildlike, venturing alone,
Ignoring Fay's penned markings on the map
And trusting to that cup of sheerest blue
To hang above a place that might be home
Or haven for a time, a resting-spot
For migratory birds who longed to find
A nest, a stay against confusion's reign.

Along the road, some houses had been burned,
Perhaps by mischief. Grass and weeds seemed thick,
And June's green leaves were plentiful on trees;
She pressed on, watchful, fearing to meet those
Who made such senseless havoc in the world,
Drifted past a blind-eyed traffic light,
Discovering that not all had been fired
And wrecked… The road dead-ended at a lake,
And Thalia jumped down, kicked off her shoes,
And fled across the lawn. A drifting boat
Enticed her eye along the shore to where
A tower rose from waves; she saw a star
That coruscated on the water's skin
But soon resolved to something humanlike
With filaments of hair and limbs of fire,
Who spoke to her in words that guised themselves
In jabs of lightning and in thunderclaps:
Childe Thalia, fear not, I bring you news
—For I am made the messenger of worlds—
That here you will reside and take your rest,
And you will be the ruler of your tribe,
Those children who accompanied you here,
And though a dereliction on the way

—For where is Gabriel, that child of light,
Who might have been the father of the world?—
Meant grievous waste and murderous affront,
Yet hark to me, one bidden in this hour
To carry balm to Thalia and say
Almighty God will give you a great gift,
Although it may be long before you grasp
Its shape, and long before you cease to learn
How lone you are against the powers who
Have ravaged town and lyric countryside.
Say nothing to the others but recall
In hours of despair the promise made.

The children found her lying by the lake,
Her body toppled by that mystic sight,
Her arms still twitching from a brush with force
And ears still ringing with those syllables,
Her eyes rolled back as if to dedicate
All seeing to the scrutiny of mind,
Investigate the winding corridors
And thread a magic labyrinth of brain.
An hour passed before she could speak words,
Declaring this the destined paradise,
Christening the village *Sanctuary*
To signal with new name a day of birth.

IX. The Thalians Choose Home

YEAR 1 AFTER THE FIRE

A door of lake, a door of glimmering, as if between two worlds.

The lakeside park was seeded with fresh graves,
A little yellow bulldozer perched high
On top a berm of earth, but every street
Seemed absent, cleansed of ordinary life.
Not wanting to abandon precious shields
And toys, the children rode about the town,
By instinct hugging close to the lakeshore,
And braked when Thalia cried out, *That one!*
Why not? So many homes, as if asleep,
Held still and silent on the empty streets.
The one she chose was lovely, neither brick
Nor stone but clapboard, yellow trimmed with white,

With generous wide porch along the front
That made them long for the lost things of home,
The porches and rocking chairs, the ceiling fans
And storytelling under wisteria,
Musk-scented scuppernongs, and orchard trees
Yielding a scent of peaches to the wind.
But what persuaded Thalia was not
A porch or craggy trees or flowered lawn:
The wide-flung door through which she saw the lake,
As if the house were sited in two worlds,
The one more commonplace, though tainted now,
The other stirring with odd glisterings,
A sea-gray, restless, moody atmosphere—
The door of glimmering suggested peace
And joys that wake beyond apocalypse
To hopeful Thalia, a happy end
As sometimes in a half-forgotten play
Unearthed and acted on a village green,
Where actors in a troop join hands to sing
And scenes of tragedy rehearse their close
In measures that turn tragi-comedy.

The breezes from the lake came murmuring
Through open windows in that night of calm,
And children slept, their bodies drifting free
Of journey's toil, anxiety, and fear
As if they floated in the water's depths,
Made weightless in a buoyant, chasmal jade.
At dawn they awoke with a dreamy sense
Of something set loose from the bounds of land,
The house a spacious boat that sat between
The earth and sky, the water and the town,
A wanderer that yet might sail away
To other worlds and navigate by stars
Unseen by human eyes until an hour

When six remaining children glimpse a sky
Where unfamiliar constellations rule
A dazzling zodiac—the Nine-tailed Cat,
The Throne of Fire, the Fount of Anguishing,
Un-mercy's Seat. I might go cruelly on,
But I have brooded for too long on fall
And desolation, hidden history
Of world's end, thing unwritten in the books,
Its causes and its powers scribed on air
And seen out of a corner of the eye
Or not at all. Better to dream and say
That sparkling zodiac shows sympathy
For trial and weariness, presenting Hope
In Silver Feathers, Gabriel in Light,
The Mother's Arms, the Father's Sailing Boat,
The Seven Triumphant Against the Waste.

X. Stranger

Year 1 After the Fire

The morning brought surprise, along with news of how the village fared.

The morning mist came rolling from the lake
To snare in trees and drift across the lawn,
Snagging on the long grass and the flowers,
A waist-high cloud that blurred the borderlines
Between the water and the earth: a man
Was standing in the bull's eye of the yard.
They sprinted to the windows, stared from shade
Of damask curtains at the watcher who
Without a word was waiting in a hush
That seemed a kind of patience to the ones
Who peered and breathlessly described his looks—
Ancient to them, and old to those who live
The metamorphosis of dwindled life,
Though we who are the lesser in our years
May dive deeper than those who came before
Who wasted inwardness and soul on things
That glance at surface, dissipate, dissolve
And leave no writing on the page of mind.
Yet Thalia, our eldest one, remains.

The six soon ventured to the dew-streaked porch,
Elaine and Alexandra clinging fast,
Each to the other, Samuel made bold
By thinking on his father's bravery
And how he locked the evil ones in jail,
Ran easy, hardly pricked by fearfulness
That might disturb the equanimity
Of thoughts still flotsam on the tide of sleep,
Fay praying underneath her breath for aid,
Discernment of the right to say and do,
With Thalia beside, her courage warm,
Awakened from its slumber by the need,
Strong-hearted nature stirring at the call.
The children moved together through the grass
And cloudiness that seemed uncertainty
Of earth—they searched for clarity and signs
That though this was a man, he would not hurt.

Who shattered morning's silence into shards?
Unknown, though history records the gist
Of storytelling words the stranger spoke:
I hoped, I thought you might be some of mine,
My family, or people who once lived
Within the precincts of this little town
And who might know the news of those I've lost,
Misplaced and yet will find, I'm sure of that—
I was away from home the day of fire
When all the world became burnt offering
To the old foolishness of restless men
And had much trouble gaining home again.
The village had been emptied of its life,
The living having gone to safer ground
Or so they thought, deluded by that hope,
And many dead lay spilled around the park,
A crowd of concert-goers, young and old,

The elderly expecting death some day
But not that day, others in prime of life,
Some shielding babes and toddlers in their arms,
The circling children fallen at their game,
Their ring-around-the-rosy touched with ash,
And on the bandstand, our musicians sprawled,
Sceptered with gold and silver instruments.
I buried all in earthen tumuli
Akin to tombs of Stone Age kings and queens
Who ruled beyond the sea—bulldozing dirt
On lawn-chair thrones and horns and shining flutes
That nevermore would breathe a note of song.
And when the noise of laboring was done,
The silence ruled until a gang of boys
Invaded, torching homes forefathers built.
I crept through backyards to the station house,
In darkness sought the generator's pulse
And sounded the alarm for fire—not once
But many times until my ears seemed bells.

The caravan of those remaining—who
Knows where the cars and people fled to find
Some safer place? There is no safer place
Than this, no sweet untainted Arcady
With crystal streams and orchards flowering,
Without a jot of poison in the cells
Of fruit that ripens in the summer's heat,
So if not here, there is no place for us,
Where we may live our shortened lives in peace,
Or close enough. There is no peaceful land,
And gates of Eden long ago clanged shut…

The children, longing for authority
And conscious of the gulf between themselves
And sixty-three, were formal in address—

They liked the titled name of *Doctor Thorn*
As somehow reassuring to their fears
And followed him to learn about the town,
Those portions still unburned—the hospital
And stores, the streets that cut between the two,
The shore where boats still bobbed at anchorage.
He called himself the chatelaine of all,
The keeper of the locks—had spent some days
In searching for the keys to doors of shop,
Hotel, museum, house, and hospital,
Collecting for some future life the rooms
That might be wanted by his villagers.

Then Thalia, as ever prescient,
The one elected queen among her peers,
Though blushing at her own temerity,
Demanded from him anything he knew:
To teach us what you can of medicine
And how to cure a wound, and how to staunch
Its blood, and how to save a pregnant girl
From the death in childbirth dooming women
In older centuries that now recur
Or seem to haunt us with their crudity
And naked ignorance—though they had taste
To make their selves more beautiful than ours
In golden ages, or so I have dreamed;
I am a child but do believe the years
Have been unkind to things that matter most,
And maybe we can make a finer world,
One more alive with beauty, where the soul
Can flourish like a tree beside a stream
Despite the poison cast like shadow leaves
From canopies of boughs made pale with ash.

Then Doctor Thorn made promises to each
That though he meant some day to wayfare north
And find his daughter's camp in wilderness
To join that branch of family once more
—If they were there, if only they were there—
Before he died, he'd not go journeying
Until they did not need him as a guide,
That he would pass on learning till they held
More than sparse rudiments of medicine
And also knowledge of the pharmacy,
Understanding what was safe prescription,
And what would soon transform to be no use.
He pledged restoring help to make a world
Of mathematics and of literature,
Of roofs and furnaces, of water, wood,
Pipes and lines and back-up generators.
In idle hours, he liked to hunt for bear
And delve for pike, and bound himself to teach
The lore of firearms, how to hit a mark
And oil and swab a gun with bristled bronze—
He practiced archery, for country men
Were fond of shooting like some Robin Hood
In thickets or from rafts aloft in trees,
And capable to hang and dress a deer,
To butcher venison and cure a skin.
Then Sam was pleased and eager to acquire
A hunter's lore of tracking, stealth, and aim,
And Ran already had acquired a pride
In doing useful things with awl and plane,
For he could do some simple carpentry
And often he had helped to tend the store,
To stock a wood-hoard with sweet-smelling pine,
To shunt the gleaming nails in bins by size.
But Fay was lured by books and library,
And wanted to explore a nearby church

For music sheets, perhaps for wine and host
Made blessed by priests before the laving fire—
The twins, devoted company of two,
Locked arms, declaring they were satisfied,
Whatever was decided by the rest.

Surprised by strong intent, the children chose
To school themselves for resurrected life,
To save their days from want and winter's cold,
And though they often quarreled, played the fool,
And leap-frogged work on sudden holiday,
Ransacking Main Street shops for toys and games
Or picnic jars and bottles to uncork
Beside the lake when *Marco Polo* palled,
Most daily hours of learning sailed away,
And everything they treasured up seemed good
For use or understanding, or to make
The labor on the way alive with joy,
With pictures, tales, and songs that drive the heart
Distracted with delight, enchanting them
Until the mortal storehouse was as starred
And rich as Ali Baba's cave with gems.

XI. The Rebel Sky

Year 3 After the Fire

Elaine and Alexandra drifted to the idyllic heart of the lake,
and the blue-black roses of the sky consumed the halcyon day.

Pure tedium's a blessing to the one
Whose anguish has been metamorphosis.
It would be pleasant then to fancy years
Unspooled in calm without more suffering,
That all the children had to do was breathe
And work in sweet content and merriment
That comes despite the losses in a life;
I'd rather sing that changeless dream of peace…

One morning when the winter had withdrawn,
When spring had fled the bursting green it birthed
And given place to high midsummer's heat
That made the children weary in their tasks
And fretful at the yoke of Doctor Thorn

(Each day the atmosphere grew jellied-strange
As pressure screwed the threaded lid of sky
Atop the land until a genii force
Erupted from the bottle of the world,
Shattering air with jam-dark thunderstorms,
Stunning earth with blasts of pearly hailstones,
Cleansing sky with lightning bolts and deluge,
Then shutting up the racket-skirl in hush,
Disintegrating cloud, and tranquil blue),
A little boat appeared—a tempting shape
Sunk deep in water, with a threadbare sail,
And Alexandra and Elaine swam out
To see what pleasure boating might afford,
Two mirrored nymphs who glided on the lake.
I've hardly told the chronicle of twins
Who spent the day in effervescent tune,
Their voices making counterpoint to Fay's
Like birds that arc and swing above the gulfs
Of northern lakes deep-gashed by glacial ice.
In heritage they were Americans
Who send their roots and tendrils far and bloom
All multifarious in eye and skin,
A sort of cottage garden of the world;
These two were blossoms on a grafted tree,
Resembling each the other one as much
As one silk thread resembles another,
But strong because the days demanded strength
And grown in knowledge of those needful things
Required by those who must remake a world.

The dappled, leaf-strewn shallows near the shore
Appeared so mild the others hardly knew
How the current eased the little sailboat
So gently from the sands until it swerved
In stronger currents to the lake's blue heart.

A single seagull, blown across the land
In trailing the St. Lawrence seaway's course,
Made antic flutterings around the mast
And screamed a warning to the girls, who laughed
At its distress and waved when Thalia
Made giant gestures from the beach to say
They should return before the afternoon
Transformed itself with plungings of raw night
From devilish thunderheads and bolting stars.

The two were singing, voices swallowed up
By distance and by trellised heat that soared
And set its navy roses on the sky
To darken shore and lake with burgeoning
Of petals packed with icy seeds of hail.
False twilight crept inside the streaming grass
As Samuel raced pounding up the street
To search for Doctor Thorn, who had revealed
So many mysteries, but not of boats
And sailcraft, tiller, rudder, how to row
Without spinning in a useless circle,
Though with his aid the children salvaged boats
And wrestled them ashore because a boat
Had once been savior to the drowning world.

The roses blossomed on heat's lattices
In blues no earthly rose could conjure up—
Great cabbage roses, bruising cumulus
With pearly dew that sluiced the prickled stems
And, sliding on cold streams within the air,
Vaulted from a moveable precipice
To slam from heights on wind-lashed surfaces
As lightning's forests sprouted upside down.
Somewhere impossible to breathe and be,

Where cataracts are ring-tailed roarers seized
And then let go, where hail is grown from dust
Like instant pearls to rattle in the sky.
A power struck war hammers on the rose
And rock of anvil-clouds: the rain obscured,
Erased the land, ascended as a mist.

A mocking rainbow linked the lake to sky
As Doctor Thorn set out with Thalia
And Samuel to rescue the lost twins,
The gusts of wind had scooped and thrust the boat
Close to the tower by the eastern shore,
And Doctor Thorn recounted how and why
The folly had been raised to please the rich
And keep the masons occupied in years
When stonework seemed too rich and costly-high
For ordinary pockets... Syllables
Blew back in wind. The low-slung sailboat lay
Heeled to one side, and though they shouted names,
A silence scarved the place with muffling mist,
And Alexandra and Elaine, the twins
Pristine and perfect in their youthfulness,
Who should have been the mothers of the world
Were staring open-eyed into the lake
That thunderstorms had switched from steady blue
To jade: their bodies bare, not far apart,
Arms curved like wings, their fingertips still close,
As if the twins had still been holding hands
Until they could hold nothing anymore.

XII. The Face of Light

YEAR 3 AFTER THE FIRE

The peace of graves, with Thalia as raging as a storm-raked sky…
And when she reproached God, the angel with the broken face replied.

The girls were tucked in earth, their arms entwined,
Their hair still damp from what the old man called
His *Glimmerglass*, the looking glass, the lake
Of moods and wind that sometimes thrashed the trees
Till squirrels came slinging, hurtled from a branch
And catapulted into rain-drenched air.
The day was cool, the loveliness of earth
Increased by rain that made green greenier
And brought its deepening to lawns set free,
Old-fashioned blossoms tangled in the weeds
And wildflowers that hung in bells and stars
Among the churchyard graves that bore with grace
Two hundred years unchanging quietude.
But Thalia, unquiet, ranged the aisles

And ranted in her discontent and rage
Against the speechless ways of God & Son:
I'd like to be a Xerxes, flog the waves
To punish water for its faithlessness!
How did their gentleness, their harmlessness
Offend? Why couldn't You who walked the waves
For sport and joyousness while fishers cried
Aloud to see the water towering
As if to strike the moon, then slammed to foam,
Why couldn't You have reached a hand to save,
A palm of air with fingers that could cup
A tiny boat and swing it safe ashore,
A hand of dovelike wings to waft the lost,
A hand made fatherly and motherly
To those who had no parents to defend
From wild and sudden witless thought that sailed
Them into death? Why couldn't You be kin
And kind to those who suffered pains to bring
The newborn world from remnants of the old,
Who were the phoenix on its nest of ash?
Annealed in glass, the molten figures burned
In summer light and seemed to waft on gloom,
The eyes of saints and angels knowledge-stained.
The green arch of a doorway to the yard
Made up another Gothic pane of light,
And chalices and crosses shed stray glints
Along the sweep of marble altarpiece.
A skein of crumpled leaves stirred by the wind
Made helpless flutterings around her feet.
The angel with the missing face let in
A blast of beams and, brightening, lit up
The church as Thalia said, *Once I heard*
A voice: you made a promise to me then,
A girl who now has failed her promises
And lost—so careless—Gabriel and twins,

But I am only human and a child
(Or would be child in different days than these—
Now I am something stranger than a child,
A sort of woman, child alert too soon,
And am responsible for much—too much
For humankind to manage and endure),
While You, if You exist, are God of this
And every other world and universe,
The fused creative force of artistry
That tossed this ball of Earth and fretted it
With fjord and lake and jagged rock and cloud,
Who animates the dove and infant child
And streams in flame across the firmament,
And so I hold You to that promise made
In winged prophetic bonfire on the lake,
For I can keep no promise but break all
And strive again to keep some covenant
With life and death within a ruptured world.
The sunshine made a starburst where the head
That lay in dreamy pieces on the floor
Once shone, auroral work of Tiffany;
The star face brought a lightening of flesh
To Thalia until the piercing rays
Transformed her body into starriness,
And rain of light made reign of light within,
Till she was drowned and nameless in its flood,
And there with trembling let the angel speak
At first as if she heard a shell-cupped voice,
And later on as if a bell had clanged,
And last in speaking silence that could shake
The body, drive it onto knees in glass.

Remember in the shadow of despair
What you have known: the messenger of fire
Who burned with syllables on water's skin,

For God is otherwise than what you dream
And knew your secret name before the shear
Of light, explosive kiss that birthed the stars
And juggled planets in their whirling course—
He calls your glowing name and bids you rise,
No matter if the universe is scorched
Right to the root a thousand thousand times,
For you must still be phoenix to the world.
Again she heard her name as in a shell,
The echoes fragmenting in corridors
Of nacred pearl—she walked its labyrinths,
Pursuing through the shining halls and rooms
The quiet steps of someone like a star,
And when she woke on blades of glass and leaves,
The taste of blood was acrid in her mouth
And world seemed muted, sluggish like a dream
In which our limbs are helpless, stayed by force
Of something powerful and yet obscure.

XIII. An Unexpected Arrival

Year 67 After the Fire

Emma muses the ways of epic tales, far-fetched and long ago,
beginning with a journey or beginning with a stranger come
to town, as now a stranger slipped into her library: her life.

I wonder if there's any famous tale
Long told around a bonfire's flickerings
That did not link its ancient measurings
Or else more modern feet to restless feet
Departing or arriving—portals clang,
The famous warrior, scaled and barbed in bronze,
Shatters the atmosphere within a hall
Where thanes and chieftain have been schooled to sweat,
Awaiting worst that grisly monsters do,
Or a girl lingers by the maw of hell,
Irresolute and trembling in the gloom,
Or some strange enmity of gods delays
A man from harbor till he learns the path
Across the water-fields comprises all
The life he ever had, with love and war
And mystery of salt, unfathomed seas
Where isles of home become Elysian,

Or something streaks across the onyx air,
The vertical wild fire of Lucifer
Slung down from heaven while the fallen moil
Like moths around his incandescent light.

As potent as a warrior in my way
—A singer of the founding matriarch,
A slayer of the slavering pack hounds,
Defender of the book and document,
A quester charged to liberate the page—
I come and go with gun and leathern shield
And sword against the streets and wilderness.
And though I've fought a madman in the hills
And battled shrieking rats as big as dogs,
I am no Thalia with heart to strike
Almighty God if He offended her.

A stranger came to town this afternoon—
He was not here, and then at once he was.
I saw him standing on the portico.
A reflex tightened fingers on the knife
Bound at my waist, and yet I lifted up
The window-sash, invited him inside,
Where he looked round in wonder at the books
And cases lined with painted manuscripts,
Then laughed to find *librarian* a word
That still had meaning in a splintered world.
His eyes were green as Glimmerglass in storm,
His hair was yellow, bound with strips of rag,
But carelessly, befitting to a man
Unconscious of his looks. Alone a year
After his mother died her wasting death,
He left in search of life. *So magical,*
These things you have collected and heaped up
Like dragon's treasure. So, so marvelous.

His eyes moved from the gold-leafed interlace
That made a page transform to labyrinth—
I wished to keep him snared inside those coils,
To place my palm against the flush of skin
Along a cheek, but news cannot be hid,
And so the Grand High Mayor of our town
—My sister Gaby, mother seven times,
Appointed years ago by Thalia—
Has stolen him away for questioning
About his skills, for poring over maps,
For news a traveler can lend to us,
The sparkle of the water and the air
In distant lands, and where the hunt is prime
Or else not worth the price of journeying,
To learn if he is peaceful in his bent,
Whether courtesy and civility
Are sweet to him, and whether he could be
Content and glad to be a Thalian.
My sister gazed at me and gave a nod
As if to say she knew my inmost mind
And had a tenderness for what this man
Might come to be with passage of the days—
I touch the case where fingerprints are cloud
To mar its pure transparency and dream
Of times to come and possibility
Before I yield and turn to Thalia
And Fay and Samuel and Ran who kept
Transforming as the years skimmed swiftly by.

XIV. Sands in the Hourglass

CIRCA YEAR 5 AFTER THE FIRE

*Here Emma strives to grasp the transformations coming with the years—
four, once children, wakening to earthly and unearthly longings.*

So let's be six forever and ever...
Now they were four and seldom thought of days
When they had lived as part of families
Or mourned that ill-starred instant when they set
Griefstruck Gabriel on highway pavement
And drove away. Now Samuel grew tall,
His eyes tranquillity, the hair grown long
And out-of-fashion with the former times,
(For in these years there is no fashioning
Except that need or beauty shape a thing
To an enduring form of usefulness
To please the body or renew the soul),
A quiet boy except he liked to sing,
And often he and Fay would entertain

The others with duets since she could play
The grand piano in the front parlor,
And sometimes they would tinker with the pegs
To tighten strings and tune a sour note
With manuals that Thalia rescued
While foraging for books—she early grasped
The need to resurrect the world through words
That taught them how to staunch a leaking roof
Or keep the silent organ in the church
From ruin or preserve a garden's fruit.
Whenever Fay swept through the living room
And Sam was there, his eyes were drawn to hers,
For she grew lovely with the passing years,
The child whose too-long limbs had been all twig,
The girl unkempt, uncombed, her hair in snarls,
Was womanly and moved with gracefulness.
She kept the calendar and marked the days,
And once a week they pilgrimed to the church
And listened to her read the liturgy
And preach, as Thalia had asked, because
They meant to live in high civility,
Renewing all of ancient courtesy,
Restoring all of good that had been lost,
Repudiating all with taint of wrong,
Though renaissance is difficult to find,
If not impossible for humankind.
And yet the fantasies of youth aspire
And strain for greatness if the times allow—
The dark-lit powers of the media
That spoke in lies of glossy jargonese
And raised a Tower of Babel in the mind,
The powers of the university
That fell like ivory Lucifer in dark
Of sterile hatreds, ideology,
Forgetting every joy of creation,

Hating the good, the true, the beautiful,
Disenchanting art and literature,
The powers of a giant marketplace
That demonlike bent children to its will,
The falsity infesting state and church
And all a clear-eyed watcher criticized
Had been swept clean by a corrosive broom
Of fire: now Thalia dreamed dreams of hope,
To make the golden world ancestors wished
But failed to build, or only here and there.
And yet I gaze through time at them and long
To warn them that the beautiful can die,
That good is perishing, that truth endures
But often is invisible to those
Who need it most. I would be motherly
With help of hindsight, heal the world of woes,
But might as well be made Polonius,
A prater of worn saws to younger ears.
Like Doctor Thorn's, my sage advice would be
Unheard at times, forgotten, followed now
And then… How elderly I feel, and am
Surprised, recalling I am but nineteen!
The years have blinked away since Thalia
Appointed me as high librarian,
Book-forager, the bard to weave a tale,
And as I write, I sense the living flesh
Hardening to lustrous statuary
Until I struggle to embrace their flaws
And features through the barriers of time.
The girls were likely to be listeners
Compared to Samuel, and I suspect
That Ran, intoxicated by his strength,
Alive with all of youth's exuberance,
Made wretched work of heeding Doctor Thorn
Or anyone—his copper hair curled up

As if escaping vital energies
Were dancing in a halo round his head.
He liked to spar with shield and rag-bound sword
Against the others for some petty prize
Or shoot at targets with a bow or gun
In vying to be best among the four.
Then he was happiest when others failed,
So he could master tasks—to hoist a weight
Or coax refractory machines to life.
But Thalia, the smallest of the four,
The youngest one, the slightest of them all,
Still clasped the Sanctuary leadership,
Defacto ruler of the infant town.

XV. Doctor Thorn

Year 6 After the Fire

A summer's day on Glimmerglass—departure of Grandfather Thorn.

A summer came when they could hardly be
Called children still—since fire, eleven is
The line between a minor and adult,
The year when leaders of the Clave will meet
To meditate the nature of a child
Together with the needs of family
And mandate a vocation for the life
That till then was a roving picaro,
Left free to poke a nose in anything,
To fluster fowls inside the chicken coop,
To cast transparent threads into the deep
And haul up silver flitterings of fish,
To forage in surrounding towns for food
And pause, astonished in a lightless shop
By remnants of the weird and beautiful,
To copy for the Scribe and gain a hand,
To deck the words with plants and animals.
That summer Doctor Thorn spoke his farewell,
For he had transferred what he grasped of lights

And generators, woodstoves, water pipes,
And more to them, and every house that stood
Had long ago been drained of liquid, locked
To suffer brunt of winter's snow and ice
Till rooms made clapperless were called to ring
With cries and laughter of new family.
He trusted hoops of keys to Thalia
To make her chatelaine of homes and cars
And all the village groceries and shops.
Surprised to find that a reluctant sage,
Impromptu teacher, solitary forced
To be the mentor of young wanderers
Had made himself essential in her heart
(Grandfather to the child no father knew,)
Thalia proposed they journey outward,
To paddle to the end of Glimmerglass
And travel far before they said good-bye,
For Doctor Thorn was steady in resolve
To hike two hundred miles to camp—to pack
A gun and bow, add lightweight foods and gear,
And go on quest, he said, adventuring
And unafraid of highway banditry
That might exist—or not—an obstacle
Too fierce for one so elderly as he.
Perhaps he was the oldest in the world!
He did not fear the coydogs, coyotes,
The wolf or panther, summer bears with cubs
But saved his caution for the deeds of men.
One perfect day they floated down the lake
In guideboats pilfered from a museum,
The golden shapes as graceful as new leaves:
Ahead lay winding shore, Kingfisher's spire,
Adventure, peril, chance of meeting, fair
Or ill… In glancing back, they glimpsed the house
And porches almost hidden in the trees.

The sunshine sifted from a sky that seemed
An innocent of ash and falling fire
And knew but clouds and songbirds, swaths of blue,
And nothing more. They swept close by the banks
To grasp at leaves of yellow flags that Fay
Folded, then braided into coronets
—Green hoops gemmed with flags and water lilies—
And made them wear like fairy kings and queens
Who steer the skiff-leaves to woodland haunts or swirl
Along the foam to roaring waterfalls.
Kingfisher Tower crested from the waves,
No feigned illusion though it seemed to move
Nearer and nearer, an enchanter's trick
To lure these royals dressed in flower crowns
And lock them up forever in the sky...
They clambered on the steps and thumped the door,
But no one answered—if he slept within,
The wizard needed an almighty knock
To wake the birdcage of his wands and bones
And set his spirit tweedling songs of life—
And so they waded by the rocky beach
And set their crowns to bobbing on the lake,
Skipped wave-worn pebbles, picnicked on the grass.

XVI. The Dancer in the Flame

YEAR 6 AFTER THE FIRE

When Thalia was seized by foretelling but never spoke her dream,
When came a turning in the woods—farewells and, after, silences.

Nobility of mason's hand-built walls
Was grand, close up: the tower stabbed the sky
And still loomed massive at a short remove,
Then dwindled slowly to a charming toy.
The noontime sun ignited Glimmerglass
And danced inside a fire of its own make
As if a figure swirled in sequined blaze
And led them onward with its changing light—
The glare threw veils of dazzle, dazzle cast
Uncanny aura, aura beckoned dream,
And dream was drowned by day and day brought tide
Of gold in spilling flood, to flood the mind
Until no mind was minding anything
But lapping radiance, and radiance

Ruled Glimmerglass and flashing form, the form
Of something weird, making and unmaking,
Unmaking Thalia till Thalia
Was empty husk, and husk was packed with sun,
And sun was sealed in trembling dark, and dark
Arose in dreams, and dreams made lucent night.

When she awoke, head cradled in Fay's lap,
She hardly knew their faces for an hour
Until the seizing dream began to fade.
I was alone by Kingfisher, she said,
Almost alone, and then said nothing more,
Except that she had seen the angel dance
In flames along the surface of the lake
As words had gyred and jostled in her ear.
That night they planted tents beside the shore
And Doctor Thorn dispensed his medicines
And stayed beside her till she dropped asleep.
They played like children in the lake next day
While Thalia was sleeping or else watched
From shore, and even Doctor Thorn unbent
To swim and leap from promontory stones,
To duck the boys and Fay under the waves,
To fish for pickerel and largemouth bass,
Then peel green wands for roastings on the fire,
To lie, be-whiskered like a walrus, flopped
On Glimmerglass as if it were a couch,
And once, in floating far from land, he swore
That he had seen the water roiled and loops
Of an uncoiling monster, glazed and wet,
Go shining in the sun—the creature known
To generations of the villagers
Once huddled by the deep-slit glacial lake
As something glistening and strange to see
But harmless, joyous in its sunward rise,

Returning like a dream to darkened haunts
And luck to anyone who caught the sight.

Perhaps, Ran said, *It's journey luck for you,*
Although I think a better luck would be
To let me tag along. But Doctor Thorn
Just thanked him for an offer made by each,
Afraid that he was old for traveling.
The days slipped by, and Thalia was whole,
Though never gave the words the angel sent
To wander echoing inside her ear,
Never offered more about the vision
Or what the words, *alone, almost alone,*
Might mean to her. When asked by Samuel,
She said perhaps it was no more than dream.

They dragged the guideboats onto shore and walked
Three days with Doctor Thorn along the roads
Crack-crazed by ice, invaded by the weeds,
But met no other soul along the way
Except for deer and fawns, a toppling crash
That never yielded up its mystery,
And once a party of wild baying dogs
Descended plunging from a den in hills
While Samuel and Ran were butchering
A fresh-killed buck, the others staking tents—
They kept to arrows, quiet in the woods,
And made a feast of hound and venison
In celebration of the victory
That Fay named *Battle of the Forest Dogs.*
And often one of them would slip aside
With Doctor Thorn, who now felt loathe to leave
Them free of doctor's care, though they were fit
And hoarded rudiments of medicine
With how to turn a child within the womb,

To set a broken limb to join up straight,
To cleanse and salve and stitch up ragged cuts,
And other things as needful in their lives.
And yet the instant came for an embrace,
Then one for a last glimpse along the trail,
And then another for when voices died
And soughing of the leaves filled up the world.

XVII. The Bridal May

Year 7 After the Fire

*Another spring arrived, freighted with the golden dust of pollen
and Samuel and Fay were bound with shining promises.*

What illness ails a boy of seventeen?
A grass-stained illness, green with coming spring.
How came he by such green-starred malady?
All came from looking in a hazel eye.
And did he see reflections of his face?
No, all he saw was pupil widening.
And did he teeter on the brink and fall?
He teetered long but fell into abyss.
Did he resemble shining Lucifer?
In one way only, burning like a star.
And did he die, extinguished by that flight?
Oh yes, he died a death a thousand times.
What was the reason that he died, yet lived?
The lively reason that he lived for love.

The yearning Samuel pursued his Fay,
Long slender loveliness of seventeen,
And she in turn did not discourage him,
But often ran away and laughed at love
Because she feared the cautionary tales
Of Doctor Thorn and wished he would return.
Perhaps he had been slaughtered in the hills
Or else had found his daughter's family
And might be long returning home again,
If ever the old man would venture back.
In splitting lengths of oak for winter stoves,
In mending tools, in hoeing rows of plants,
In every necessary of their days,
They two shone radiant with pent desire,
And Thalia grew certain there would be
No chosen partner for her life but Ran
And told him straight that she was much too young
For bearing children—not to ask or speak
About the future till she was eighteen,
Although he argued that life might be short
In bodies cankered, sullied after fire.

Then Samuel went foraging afar
And came home with a necklace, sapphire blue,
Unmelting ice of diamonds crowning rings,
Lockets and leafy emeralds and blood
Of rubies clutched in nests of twisted gold,
A treasure chest of winking jewelry.
Some were Thalia's as foster sister,
But most he kept as gifts for pleasing Fay,
Who scolded him, for she had been content
Without the dreamy flowers, branches cast
In silver, jeweler's lavish fantasies.
If only he had kept secure at home!

He never did reveal what clawed the gash
Like jerks of lightning jagged along one arm,
Neatly sewn as Doctor Thorn had taught him.
If only, he repeated with a laugh.
If we, when we were children wandering,
Had gone as far as Patagonia
Or borrowed ships and sailed away to sea
To China, Egypt, Singapore, Japan,
Or stopped in port at Ivory Coast or Guam
Or India or islands no one's seen,
If we had come to find the world a waste
Where nothing grew and no thing held out hope,
If we had tilled a countryside of ash,
If we had eyed a land of pillared ice
And sucked on snow for all our nourishment,
If we had stumbled onto foreign thrones
Or else been captured, forced to toil as slaves,
I still would be your love, and you be mine.

And so they married in the Gothic church
With Thalia presiding like a priest
To read the liturgy and hear the vows
And write their names inside the record book
With those of many who had gone before,
And plighted troth in that ceremonial
And sacred space while saints and angels stared.
Maid of honor and best man played florist,
Picking flowers from a ruined garden,
And served as guardians of wedding peace,
Their bows and shotguns left beside the door.
Words echoed, wavering in emptiness:
And in accordance with the purposes…
First miracle at Cana, Galilee…
And in accordance with God's holy word…

To live together in the covenant…
Be faithful as long as you both shall live…
The angel with the shattered face let in
The sun and, once, a wobbling butterfly
That made a patch of white inside the room.
Beyond the doors, the end of May was gold,
Abundant living dust, persistent seed,
Such lushness as they'd never seen before
And hardly recognized for what it was—
The promise harvest years would be ahead,
For conifers and oaks, the hickories
And walnuts, spruces, pines were blossoming
And clouding air with fertile shining silt
That somersaulted in a beam of sun,
That changed the spiderwebs to something rich,
That kissed the surfaces of Glimmerglass
And turned its scalloped border into gold,
That moved across the air as if alive,
The landscape's bright epithalamion,
The simple golden wedding of the world.

XVIII. Great Wheel of Change

Year 7 After the Fire

The wilderness begins to take the village yards, the harvest comes,
And Fay is ripening as winter seals the roads and walks of home.

Reward for winter chill and lengthened dark,
The days transformed spring's gold to green—the world
Awoke each dawn to showerings of dew
And sunlit mist that lingered in the limbs
Like combings from the starry animals
That coruscated in the gulfs of sky.
Then glinting fiddles of the crickets rasped
In overgrown farm fields to serenade
High summer's *bon voyage*, while in the weeds
The pale green crickets trilled and mourned the shift
From springtime's peepers to the katydids,
Those hunchbacked living leaves, monotonous
And shrill with end-of-summer, wing-scraped calls
That shouted down the wrens and orioles.
Coyotes and foxes wandered through town
And had to be chased off, and once a bear
Came landslide-lumbering down nearby hills
And lolled in backyard orchards for a day,
To shovel shriveled cherries in his mouth,

And only gunshot blasts and shaken bells
Could make him gather up his ample pelt
And hoist the wedge of head in air to sniff
Before he ambled casually away.

Rapunzelesque, the garden corn let down
Its silken hair from towers of pale stalk
As goldenrod and purple asters bloomed,
And hornworms spoiled tomatoes with a kiss,
Each monstrous body green and innocent,
Awaiting transformation to a moth—
The sphinx, an emblem of a mystery.
The fever of the year approached its end,
And acorn faces fattened under tams,
And everywhere was plumping grain and seed.

Ran took to hunting after dogs and deer,
And Thalia was glad, for an unease
Had somehow crept inside their gatherings,
And ticklish silences became the rule
At meals or during evenings on the porch,
For Fay and Samuel were so absorbed
In being two, there seemed no room for four,
And yet another floated in the room,
Invisible and quiet, third with two,
The baby to transform their settled lives.
They had lost hope of Doctor Thorn's return
And seldom spoke of him or of their need
Except as one might mention confidence
In all that he had taught of pregnancy,
Though often Samuel reviewed the plates
That pictured infants sluicing to the light
And other things, less joyful, hard to see
For one whose happiness was pinned to one—
That is, to being two, surviving three.

The flight of milkweed floss and thistledown
Was autumn in the air, and gossamer
On dew meant parachutes of spiderlings
Had sailed across the village in the night.
All day and evening, migrating geese
Cried the news that the world was shifting fast,
That buffleheads and loons and green-winged teal
Rode on the streams of air or breezy lake
With widgeons and whimbrels and mergansers,
That every cell sang metamorphosis
And wobbling flight to monarch butterflies,
That flowers faded, whitening as flashes
Of color struck the maple trees with flame.
Though apples rumbled through the cellar door,
Fay seemed the pattern of all fruitfulness.

Then endless stars of winter sifted down,
And ice, beginning as translucent skin
That tautened on an edge of grass and stones
Shut Glimmerglass in blue that snared the twigs
And ruddy seed and falling colored leaves.
The starry ramparts of the snow grew high,
Ice-paths appeared, and fishing holes were sawn—
They cut the blue eye of a well that sealed
Each evening with the thinnest lid of ice,
And narrow tunnels to the street and shops
Were open for a while, then abandoned,
Till only trodden ruts across the yard
Remained between the glowing swells of snow,
A stay against the burial of earth,
A way to outbuildings and Glimmerglass
And mountains heaped from autumn's laborings—
Resistant hickory, with cherry spars,
Italian lilacs, hoary-headed oaks
With green-leafed, white-gemmed crowns of mistletoe,
Kentucky coffee tree that budded late

And strained the wind and fought with gravity,
Crash-landing, changing lawn to instant forest.
The outer, inner lakes were sleepy now,
The baby in the tethered boat of self
Received the air, received the daily meal,
Drank at the amniotic fluid: grew.

XIX. Water Like a Stone

Years 7-8 After the Fire

The winter brings back childhood to the four, though Fay is caught by dreams,
and shadow-phantoms make the others move uneasily through town.

December's windswept ice on Glimmerglass
Was ballroom floor, adventure's field, or road.
Then Samuel unpacked a trove of furs
And winter gear—although not Northerners
Who had the skill to swoop across the lake,
They liked to teeter on the blades and laugh
Whenever someone blundered onto ice
Or spun and dropped as quickly as the leap
Of merriment and mischief in the mind…
Ran skidded out a wooden throne for Fay,
A chair enlivened with carved fruit and leaves
That stayed beside the bonfire on the shore
Or else was thrust across the moonlit ice.
There and everywhere she seemed more inward,

Stopping wordless, hand upraised and settled
On air, with the uncellared apple held
And yet forgotten as she floated free
Of work and fear, her swelling body cauled
In foraged velvet gown and long mink coat.
The cry of winter birds, the sudden swords
And rumpled panels of the northern lights
Awoke her from a dream, and then she smiled
And played invented games with Samuel
And Ran and Thalia, as if they were
Just children for a little while, amused
By sliding smooth-worn stones across the ice
Or dragging one another on a sled
Or in the tiny craft that stood tiptoe
On a silver runner—they sailed the boat
Along the lake and lingered by the spire
Of Kingfisher Tower, the chasmal dark
Ablaze with reefs and riverbeds of stars.

In February came a thaw, then freeze,
And end of March brought trickling seep and melt,
The snow beginning to release the streets
And walks, water plunging in braided brooks
That cut a thousand grooves to Glimmerglass.
One day Ran thought he spied a shadow where
No shade should be, and one time Samuel
Was sure he saw some phantom at a door,
A shop unlocked for easy foraging,
But when they combed the rooms, could not decide
If anyone had pilfered from the shelves
Of jars and bright metallic packages.
Uncertain, they took arms, patrolled the streets,
Yet saw no trace of squatters in the town,
Nor heard the footsteps of some passer-by.
But surely we are not alone, Fay said,

And visitors might be a sign of hope,
Though each felt secretly a faint alarm
That made them guarded, watchful out-of-doors,
And Ran made evening walks his policy,
To canvas chimney tops for tell-tale smoke
And scour blank-faced houses for a clue.
But Fay had other mysteries to mull
And only idly wondered, did they fear
To show themselves, or whether they were gone,
As harmless as the leaves ferried by wind.
Then Samuel resolved to linger near
In case of danger, and he bent to books
As if he had not memorized the words
Already, as if he had not rehearsed.
And Thalia felt like the handmaiden
Of Fay, to tug her from a low-slung chair,
Fetch vitamins, dried fruit, or fresh lake trout,
Appease a craving for a bottled drink
—For pomegranate, lime, or blueberry—
She pillaged from a tiny gourmet shop.
Like Samuel, she seldom left the house
Except to fish the ice or gather wood.

Befriending Fay seemed right to Thalia,
But fitter still to serve the unborn child
And offer up a hope in things unseen.

xx. First Birth, First Blood

Year 8 After the Fire

A child is born, a daughter given at the close of wintertime
when shadows stand revealed and the world rocks between the dark and light.

The hunting knife, so worn to wavering
It seemed a blue mirage against the hand,
Was scalpel to the tightened fruit of Fay,
Unlocked the child inside the bag of womb,
Unbound the waters in the secret house,
Untied the mooring, vessels of her blood,
And severed cordage binding self with self,
To let the slippery baby slide to air,
Eyes pasted shut with vernix, nose still plugged,
Who then was swaddled in loose folds of cloth
And tucked inside a winter coat for warmth.

When Samuel and Thalia came in,
Their arms heaped high with firewood for the stoves,
They shouted out, one voice, to see the floor
Awash in red, and Fay still panting fast
Despite the knife blade sunk within her chest,
Her body desecrated and the child

Stolen—and Samuel knelt down in blood
To see if there was any saving help,
But there was none, for though he cradled her
And vowed that he would seal the wounds, she slipped
Away. The only words she spoke to him
Before she sighed and changed to breathlessness
—*Find our baby*—kept dark that mystery
That she drew inward, held within her heart
Unwillingly, until her silvery
And uncorrupted spirit flashed across
The gateway separating life from death
To walk the eerie borderlands between,
Where light sifts strangely from an empty sky
And floods go rivering from out the mouths
Of caverns carved from hills of glacial ice,
The green-blue tunnels all will navigate.

A muteness in the room lay palpable
On Samuel and Thalia, as if
The world were muffled just before a storm
When landscapes seem to wait with breathlessness
Not like her breathlessness. Then Ran called out
He'd found a glove and spattered spray of blood
On snow close by the hospital, and glimpsed
A woman crouched as if to hide… His words
Abruptly broke as he swung wide the door
To stare and fail to translate sense from scene
Of childbirth, terrible Caesarean,
With their Sophrasia bent on wandering
Beyond their compass in the realms of death.

The lust for blood awoke, and Samuel,
Arms beggared, suddenly now raced for arms,
By instinct rushing not for gun or bow
But for the swords and shields the children thieved

(It seemed another's life, so far away)
As if a blade demanded works of blade,
And jerking Fragnarach from where it gleamed
In fame above a parlor mantlepiece,
He flourished edge in air, and Ran ungyred
The rags that looped in swaddlings on a sword,
Unhooked a shield of bronze, and Thalia
—Her hope lay all in rescue of the child—
Then likewise grasped a sword of bronze and shield
Of bronze that showed in high relief a day
Of war in bronze, the sky made bronze with smoke,
The blood-drenched ground transformed to hardened bronze
Where Thetis floats a breastplate like a star
To the ethereal Achilles, gilt
With grief but marvelous and beautiful,
Protected by Apollo's promises—
Those breakable though godly promises
That shield a mortal man, the breakable.

Clanging breakneck passage over snowpack,
With young men's faces glowing furnace-bright
As if the risen blood had ignited
And showed itself a danger to the world,
They swooped across the yards of melt and mud,
And Samuel pursued two stumbling shapes
That veered across the snow as one cried out
I didn't know, I didn't know—she's mad,
So do not hurt her, do not harm, forgive—
But Ran packed up the calling mouth with bronze,
The sword-blade slamming upward till teeth flew
And shatterings of brainpan dyed the snow,
Though Thalia kept shrieking how they must
Slaughter no one but only save the child.
And though she flung her empty arms apart,
As if to be a living sanctuary

With sword and shield slung useless on her back,
She still was frightening; the woman howled
And veered toward Samuel with baby clamped
Against her breast—the flat side of Ran's sword
Knocked her legs, and she pitched headlong earthward
While Thalia scooped up the bundled form
Before the other two could feast their blades
On the stranger's winter flesh and marrow,
The breast and gut, the ringbolts of the spine,
Unselving her, unhumaning themselves,
Hacking the sacred wards of the body:
Close-pressed, crashing, the fell clamor of shields,
The crossroads, grand climacteric of blood,
Jar of womb-shatter, the rib-comb unteethed,
Janglings above corpse couch, red butcher bed,
The bronze swords wading in a swamp of flesh
Like toddlers splashing in a muddy slough,
Hell-scathers scraping blade along the bone,
Blood-spree, blood-spore rose red on snow-white yard
And no queen dreaming of a snow-white child,
Unable to conceive, all purity—
Blood-grit and gristle, orgiastic lark,
Terrible battle song of broken day,
Unwomaned atoms spattered over snow,
Time hurtling under a translucent sky
(Color of bone, tint of translucent horn)
To the hour when Cain is ever slaying
Abel in the dark eternal backward.

Nothing could have halted them from verdict
And vengeance, save angelic messengers
Arrived by unexpected thunderbolt.
A wail went out from Thalia and streamed
Across the mire, across the slough of blood,
Ascending, spreading, wind-whipped flare and fire,

A banner to the sky, a sail to lake,
A rippling in the molecules of earth,
A voice to shake the four-fold elements
And send the world-tree swaying on its root.

But then the baby struggled in its bonds,
So Thalia unwrapped the naked child
—*Thanks be to God it is alive, a girl!*—
Who weakly keened a protest to the skies
Against a coarse and brutal wakening,
Against the hunger and the April cold,
Against the loss of a warm, breathing world,
Against the winter light, and blinked her eyes
As Thalia dropped to her knees and wept.

A madness lives in evil, evil lives
In madness—crimson charnel-house on snow,
Man-maenad, blasphemy of sacrifice,
Samuel and Ran possessed by fever,
Hern-wild, stag-antlered wildness of the hunt,
Radiant-naked-virgin-blade wildness,
Artemis-let-slip-from-scabbard wildness,
Belling hound wildness, blood of Actaeon.
Grape treader legs splattered with harvest's wine,
They reveled, drunk and Dionysian,
The human mud making a wretched squelch
Underfoot, like tilling in sodden ground.
Then with the bowl of shield they scooped up blood
And flesh and water from the trampled snow,
And raised it up to the horn-colored sky
In turbulent fierce joy, warrior-hearted,
Though Thalia protested at the act,
At carnivalesque gaiety of red,
At churning pound and lift of pestle feet,
And she remembered little Gabriel

In gay confetti of their candy wrappers,
Abandon's child, alone with the immense,
And cried out for the sake of suffering
As glowering angelic light was tipped
From vertical, toppling through amber light:
In seizure's midnight, Thalia descried
Two young men tumbling from a ledge of air,
The outswept hair a nimbus, comet-fire
Extinguished in the lake, but when she drew
Close to the floating bodies, saw that twins
Were lying peacefully on waveless sky,
Hands linked and cloudless eyes reflecting blue
And then her face, made more than baby-small.

XXI. The Lake-Washed Queen

YEAR 8 AFTER THE FIRE

Then Fay is washed and made a queen, and names are given to the child,
and Thalia reproaches Samuel for laying waste to life...

Third mourning day: the battling boys subdued,
The shawl-bound baby tied to Thalia
Who perched on Fay's great throne of pregnancy,
Unwell and weak but taking hold of life,
Directing what to do—knee-deep in lake,
The others washed Sophrasia clean of blood.
The body chilled grew colder, waxier,
And tiny icebergs bobbed around her shape
As if they meant to cling and seal her fast,
Ice-coffined princess wakened by no kiss,
And afterward she lay in statued state
To water-stain mahogany with white
And make a dim, uncertain shadow girl
That even now still haunts the table-top
And calls the woman into memory.
Perfume and ointment salved the jagged wounds
And clothed the body and the hair with scent
While Samuel fetched rings and necklaces
And Thalia tugged arms in velvet sleeves,

Though all of them were needed to cocoon
The rigid Fay inside her glistening coat.
When Thalia pinned braidlets in a crown
And left the rest as curling waterfalls,
The work was done; then, young in death, Fay seemed
A very queen from out the ancient world,
One who led battle from a chariot
Of gold with steeds as marvelous as those
Achilles urged to war, that tossed off joy
In shaking their immortal floating manes,
Stamped earth until it clanged like a cymbal
But could not bear the odor of new death
—Spirit streaming out of slain Patroclus—
And whinnied as they neared the blood-caked ground.
But now she rested from the trials of day
And slept on boards in royal finery,
High and fearless past their understanding,
So proud and unafraid of death she seemed,
Her cheekbones whittled sharp, her lip up-curled,
Sweet-smelling hair in plaits and careless rings
Like labyrinths where Samuel was lost
And lost his heart and gained another one—
A woman who could make a lion heel
And come and go as tame at her command,
The secret of her wound concealed by art,
Her lake-rinsed face restored to peacefulness.

And grant her entrance into lands of light...
There is a river, streams whereof make glad
The city of God... The sun shall not burn thee,
By day, nor moon by night... If I take wings
Of morning, dwell in uttermost of sea
Even there also shall thy hand lead me...
A lamb of thine own flock... and dust to dust...
In sure and certain resurrection hope...

The fire-faced angel brightened at the words,
And in the starburst of the face, the gold
Of sunlit dust made motions of delight
Or simple idleness as Thalia
Read the burial of the dead with tears
And many stoppings to compose herself,
Remembering the flare-fall of Fay's voice
Resounding, singing in the darkened church.

The shroud of silken sheets, the baby's cry,
The chiseled grave in crystal-threaded ground,
The hacked-out trench that Thalia made Ran
And Samuel prepare for scraps of flesh
And marrow bones that once had been living,
The clotted bandage strapped around the thigh
Of Samuel, the wound nothing to him
Till Fay was sunk in glitterings of earth,
The way that he refused the little one
And let another speak the gift of names
And drip them on her head at christening—
These things were memories that Thalia
Recalled as fresh-forged grief when years had passed.

Then Samuel in sorrow vowed to her,
Now I will leave and find another place,
A village where my heart is not in earth,
And Thalia replied to him with truth:
There is no other village, is no place
To find where your dead heart is not in earth.
And still he moaned his lot, exclaimed with tears,
I want to go where ground is not a waste,
And where my life is not a ruined town.
And Thalia with mercy said to him,
In time you will begin to heal your heart
And all that seems a waste will bloom once more.
But he went on in anger, blaming God,

The strangers who had maundered into town,
The grave that meant a stone around his neck,
Until she spoke in haste against his words:
For you there is only this blood-drenched ground,
The murdered life that is your freight of guilt,
Also the murdered life that is your own,
The world that you create by how you act
Or see or how you dream the world to be,
Your world that's ruined everywhere like this,
Which you yourself have caused to be a waste,
Which you yourself have scorched with inner fire.

XXII. Three Suitors to Her Love

Years 67 and 8-9 After the Fire

*Emma mulls the luxury of suitors in Ran and Samuel
and how Thalia, the new-minted mother, gave her heart away.*

Imagine in our world to have a choice
Between two suitors—possibilities—
As now began to threaten Thalia.
But I will not repine at my sole chance,
A stranger come to town by accident
Or guidance from some angel messenger—
A thousand times I would lift up the sash
And ask him in, and later take his hands
And say *I will, I will,* for Thalians
Are short-lived candles, flaming clarity
That sees and knows the shape of its desires.
And so this village Thalia renamed
As *Sanctuary,* later still as *Clave,*
The word that names the forum of adults

That leads our village forward into light,
Appointing tasks and roles, apprenticeships
As children's natures and the need dictate,
Is like a bonfire ever fed with life
That closes up in embers' glow and ash,
Yet is renewed. So I, the Bard of Clave,
The Storyteller and Librarian,
Will bind myself forever to this man
Before the changing company of Clave
And leave the common house where Thalia
—Who must have often wished another life—
Once meditated on her choice of men.

Desiring was the most of it: the fire
And energy of youth that sets the hair
To floating round a heat-stirred face and throat
And sometimes seems as if it is the force
That juggles orbs around the spark of sun
And spins the world in daily pirouette.
Ran spoke his words with plainness, and drew her
Hard against his muscled length of torso;
She shuddered at the memory of strength
Unleashed in bloodiness on melting ice,
And the baby on her hip awakened
To separate them with a rebel wail.
Her words were as plain-speaking as his own:
I am but seventeen, so will not join
My body with a man's and risk the birth
Of children that I am too young to bear
Without a doctor or a midwife near,
Or let myself go dreaming of romance
Until my eighteenth birthday passes by
And all my promises to Doctor Thorn
That I would be a vessel sealed from men,

Unbroken, virginal till womanhood,
Are then fulfilled, and he restored to us
In skill and wisdom, as I often hope.

The baby, Sophie Fay, demanded much
From Thalia, and she was glad to yield
And carry her away from company
To rove the streets and let the hints of spring,
Appearing like the frailest haze of green
Before the headlong bursting of the leaves,
Renew a banished peacefulness of mind.
The baby gave herself to Thalia,
Adored her with a frank idolatry,
And though the foster mother longed for Fay
And, musing, dreamed a dream of revelry
Between the gleeful mother and her child
And knew such joy was never hers by rights,
She loved the child in turn as she was loved.

Some months had fled before she realized
That Ran and Samuel were bound as friends
Yet vying—one demanded that his babe
Should own a father and a mother too,
The other charged that he alone had missed
All pleasures of the bed, so had the right
To stake his flag in claim on virgin flesh
And flash with shivering from head to foot—
He would not bide until an infant girl
Was ripe enough for plucking by his hand!
Their morning sparrings in the weeds turned fierce,
With *thwok!* of blades, each swaddle-clothed in rags
And bell- and hammer-notes from walloped shields
That echoed sleepily from hills and lake.
But worst was when they kept the peace but looked
At her sidelong with avaricious stares,

As if they had a pact she might not like.
I am in charge, she vowed to Sophie Fay,
I am in charge of me and you, and no
Aggressor boy shall steal our liberty,
Though I have known them long and trusted them
Despite man-violence of berserker deeds,
And love them in a way, as sisters do,
What's loyal plaited with derisive scorn
For idiotic things that brothers do.

In halcyon days Ran and Samuel
Brothered their bond in pillaging the land
And caught the blue-black horses that became
The Eve and Adam of our equine tribe
My sister the Horsemaster rules with comb
And reins and words that horses understand.
One month they bent their minds to tinkering
And took a car to shards and back again,
Then somehow made it go and drove away
And came home soused and whooping, faces scratched,
With chickens gargling protests from the trunk.
This escapade gave Thalia a hope
That they could tame some bawling feral cow
—What baby wants her milk in little cans?—
And soon a Guernsey heifer frisked with deer
In meadows merging with the wilderness
Beside the brink of town, and Thalia
Twice daily rode a bike with Sophie Fay
Sliding behind in a wheeled carrier,
The baby chortling as if only birds
And breeze were needed to arouse her joy.
When autumn came, they fitted up a shed
To shelter cow and chickens, left the fields
And barn to horses, blue-black slender shapes
That seemed near cousins to a bird in flight,

Racing through the waist-high meadow seedheads
Or leaping up to paw at the first snow
That whirled in dervishes and made them bolt.
The pastoral of summer, falling leaves,
And endless-seeming snow spun round the year
Till crocuses of April bloomed again,
And little Sophie Fay knew naming words,
And Thalia's eighteenth birthday drew near.

XXIII. Eighteen Times Around the Sun

Year 9 After the Fire

Fragnarach is tested—truth or falsehood?—on Thalia's birthday,
and all her world is altered in a strange morning of forsaking.

The clang of metal woke her on the day
As dawn filled up the window-glass with rose,
As syllables and breath transformed to cloud:
Those nincompoops, she murmured to the air,
And curled to nap around quicksilver's child,
Alchemic, changing to a little girl
Who talked her seven lilting words and scaled
The staircase on her hands and knees, and liked
The ice or lappage of the lake so much
That she went nowhere without someone near.
The noise—irregular, staccato-chimed,
Cymbaled and slammed, grotesque and musical—

Battered her drowse and jangled Thalia
Awake with a barbaric din of steel:
So this is what they meant by a surprise!
Then, stiff with cold, she clattered down the stairs
And out-of-doors where Samuel and Ran
Were lunging, parrying with naked swords
Inside a red-tinged cloud of morning mist,
Cocoons of rags and bindings to the blades
Shucked, raveled on the greening April earth.

Hawk-throated shrieks of havoc jarred the air
As blood made branching, silent rivulets,
And Glimmerglass seemed hushed with ebbing dawn,
A few panes sliding over retted ice
And waves behind the house—the open lake
That seems eternal flashing in the sun
With crowns of blue or ice and yet: is not.

And neither one would harken to reproach
Or reason but berserk and foaming wheeled
To hurtle her across the thawing ground
And slashed again, so daubed in muck that she
Hardly told one warrior from the other,
As if they were twin children of the dawn,
Made in the egg of cloud their swords now tore
In floating shreds, as if they were new-hatched
And bleeding, Castor-Pollux, brother chicks
From self-same nest, or even more, the same,
The very same, a mirroring in red,
And one time when the slippery wet soil
Meant sudden topplage from the vertical,
They knelt and scrambled for the blood-slick shields,
Exchanging each in flip-flop turnaround.
Perhaps they were thus equals in the fight
And would have battled endlessly and tied
If April's footing had no treachery,

But Ran, while thrusting forward, snicked his blade
On Samuel's bare throat, pitched violently
In catapults of gravity to slam
And sheath the other's sword inside his chest,
Then stare and grasp the crosspiece in his hands
And drop his head as if in prayer: and die.

So Samuel bowed down, unsheathed the sword,
And staggered to the ground—for Ran, wild-thrown,
Had punched the other's belly with his sword.
Here's Fragnarach, he said, *that cannot lie,*
And you will have a man, the worthiest
In all the fallen world, as is your right
For you are highest of the beautiful,
A girl who might be magicked petal-fall...
And Thalia, who wished to upbraid men,
Dismantle senselessness with bursts of word,
Was forced to trade rebuke for outsize woe,
Yet race for tools and thread for surgery,
And hear him weep for *Fay, my lovely Fay*
Till morphine stopped his mouth from mutterings,
Then clamp and stitch and long for Doctor Thorn,
And in the end be reconciled that she
Had done her uttermost, and afterward
She saw that Sophie Fay was fed and clean
Before she sponged the living, washed the dead
With cold lake water, sluicing Ran and swords
And shields until the ruddy water pooled
And metal sparkled in the birthday light.
And you, she cried to fresh-rinsed Fragnarach,
I fear that you have learned in time to lie,
Or else are nothing like a Fragnarach,
But are a common peasant in disguise
As something chivalrous and truth-telling.

The landscape was reflected in a shield,
Ran's favorite, caught up by Samuel,
A pastoral round window, elegant,
As human things of craft and use can be.
She lifted it and viewed the gleaming world
All cleansed of death, the boys invisible
Except as blurs that might be sheep or stones…
And set it down and did the usual
—She fed the scuttling chickens, milked the cow—
That in the face of the unusual
Must still be done, must be the usual.

Last she remembered to release the dog
And filled the water bowl and combed her fur
Close by the sleeping shape of Samuel,
Now tucked for warmth inside a mummy bag.
Would all her world contract to Sophie Fay?
And like some demon necklace, could this grief
Increase in weight, hang millstones at her throat?
Why couldn't they have waited for her choice?
But neither was the biding kind—it was
The night before when Ran and Samuel
Competed in their gifts, from Samuel
A mesh of gold made glittering with stars
That played and shifted, snatching light, or hung
In burning stillness from a crown of gold
And diamonded her hair; from Ran, a dog
Culled from a pack and hidden, tamed to come
And go, to stay or sit, defend on cue—
A red-gold creature combed to silkiness.

She fetched a rocking chair, a gun, a bow,
And heaped a bonfire close to Samuel.
The red-gold dog curled up beside the flames

And dozed, and Sophie Fay dropped off to sleep,
And everything but Thalia and stars
Was sleeping in the village; nothing stirred
To fright her watch, to make her lift the gun
Or nock an arrow on the line of gut,
Though pain was in her like a tautened string.
Once Samuel woke up to say he heard
A voice that called his name, *O Samuel!*
And later that he heard his name again,
And later still he grew confused and said
The voice was calling Ran. Perhaps it is
The voice of God, said Thalia, or else
Some messenger. He slept, awoke, and cried
For *Ran, Ran, Ran* until she cradled him
And put aside all rancor at men's ways
To say with tenderness, *My Samuel,*
My brother and my friend. Now go to him,
Go to our brother Ran and say that all
Is forgiven. And see your sleeping child?
The angel with the face of light will care
For us… Now go in peace. And so he went.

XXIV. In the End, Beginning

Despite disaster and regret and dreams of how the world might be,
now Thalia resolved to live and bring up Sophie Fay in joy.

The bodies lay neglected in the night,
But in the morning Thalia gave thought
How she might fitly rue this waste of youth
That now was only waste, imagining
These brothers floating on the lake like kings,
Their bodies splashed with oil, their garments soaked—
At twilight sliding forth, a moving flame
That roared through logs and tinder raised as tent
Above the shapes of Ran and Samuel
And slowly navigated through remains
Of winter's glow, ice islands of the moon.
Yet lake's not sea: no vesseled fire would seem
To sail and vanish in the limitless,
Nor would she drink the water from the lake
Without some fear that atoms of the two

Might dance within her glass—remembered how
Histories of archaic days confessed
That bodies of the dead were sometimes found
In kitchen middens near a settlement
And thought of that as being easiest,
To drag them to the midden near the house
And read the proper words for burial,
And do no more. But finally she built
A hill of gravel, wood, and foraged sacks
Of topsoil, though she raged against the dead
And wept and railed as if they were alive
To heed her strong upbraidings: *Tumulus
Ran-Samuel* that bulks beside the yard,
Still a mute reminding mass of earthwork,
Macabre and ancient-seeming chambered mound.

Nine days of mourning at her laboring
Until the dark, unwieldy barrow stood
Compacted by the boots of Thalia
And sprinkled heavily with seeds that lured
The birds… She read the rites for burial
And paced the floor at church with Sophie Fay,
Recalling her first visit to the place
And how they six were hushed, alarmed by glass
And by the angel with the broken face.

His perfect plumes of amethyst with smoke
Ascending, indigo, from twilight's heart
Now drew her gaze again: *And all my luck,*
She cried, *has gone amiss till blasphemy
And writhing thoughts too terrible to name
Pluck at my mind, make ruinous what once
Rose up as peace… Shall Thalia unbend
To curse the sunlight for the works of men*

And lay her rankling blame where blame is none?
And yet I wonder at the evil chance
That nearly stripped me of what matters most.
Perhaps the sin of Gabriel, forlorn,
Abandoned on the track, has weighted us
Like pocket stones in deepening water,
In spite of God's forgiveness. Could that be?
Why must I die alone, or wield the bow
And gun and sword in this bewilderness?
Before the angel's face, I now devote
Myself to something better than this dread
That clings to me like mist and memory,
For I will live and raise this child in joy,
Defying loss and fear with gaiety.

The bare-faced tumulus grew green with grass,
And Thalia renewed the winter's store,
Chopping, splitting wood, collecting tinder
And foraging for wares, though when it rained
The library was home—that year she roved
Its wayward jumble, finery and junk,
And read of plumbing, woodstoves, hand-laid stone,
Hunting and fishing, ways of animals,
Read storybooks to little Sophie Fay
And Red, the glossy dog, and slashed a trail
Through lyrics, monstrous epic tales in verse,
And plays she furbished with gilt theatres
Of mind, with comedy or tragedy,
Romance or history, rainbowed or dark,
And tales with cities and technology
Or pastorals of dreaming countryside
Or something long ago and faraway
Or once upon a time, all strange to her.
Yet what, she mused, *could be so strange as this*

Abandoned village in the Northern wild,
The rippling loops of monster in the lake,
Kingfisher Tower spiring over ice
Or waves, the Norman tower in the woods
The boys once found, exploring on horseback—
And we could live near sky, be unafraid,
Warded by walls of stone, and let the wolves
Tick nails across the frozen lake to howl
And scare the white-faced O of moon, not us,
Secure and happy in our castle walls…

The winter fell down piecemeal from the clouds,
But Sophie Fay and Thalia were snug
At home with books and kindled fire and Red,
With Thalia beginning now to dream
Her life might be, if not a comedy,
Then not entirely tragedy, two masks
That groaned and laughed, a Janus head in stars
That fell the winter long until the melt
Made streams and swelled above the waterline,
The causeway to the tower lost. She said,
Impossible to think that one of us
Is last in all our world when spring is new.
How sad, when I am ready now to help
The world be born, and when I daydream tales
Of Clave remade to hold my family.
I call it Clave, she whispered to the child,
This village echoing with emptiness,
This harmless make-believe of family,
Where I am queen and rule with equity
And wisdom as in fairy tales where all
Can end with new beginnings of delight.
I feel a power in me like the melt
That quenches fire and heals the world in spring,
Yet all for nothing if nothing is all
Will husband me and breed a family.

She held the toddler up to show her how
The snow ran melting into pores of earth
Till water sopped the soil and flooded parks
And put out fire, forever and ever…

One springtime morning bluish spirals meant
Tendrilous smoke beside Kingfisher Tower.
Scent floated from the ground and over lake,
Where shimmers of an infant green had touched
Drooping willow withies at the margin,
Poplar catkins, and tassels on the oaks,
While green-up seized the grass and violet leaves.
Last evening's mist dissolved into the air,
And on the flood-high surface of the lake,
The angel light was brightening in trance.
So Thalia went out with sword and bow
To load the paddles, ready the canoe
And took the dog and child, who fell asleep,
Rocked by waves, and when she neared the tower
She saw the maple trees were dense with cloud
As if with the most delicate new leaves,
Saw, ankle deep on causeway stones, a man
Gleaming with water, rinsing face and throat.
The little boat slid near as he stood up,
His hair a splash of bronze against the mist,
And something of him like a shape foreknown.

He called to Thalia, *My name is Thorn.
My grandfather sent me.* She laughed and said,
I thank him for the gift, for she was glad,
Renewed in hope, and suddenly she knew
As prophets know in light-drenched prophecy,
Finally the age of fire had ended
Along with winter, sluiced by springtime rains,
And now began the green-up time for Clave,
With dreams of branches leafed in family,

A newfound father for the fatherless,
A green that shimmered, barely out of reach,
With springing spate to flood the winter land,
With cloudy limbs and dances of the sun.

All praise to Mother Thalia and Thorn—
Here sprang the new beginning to the world.

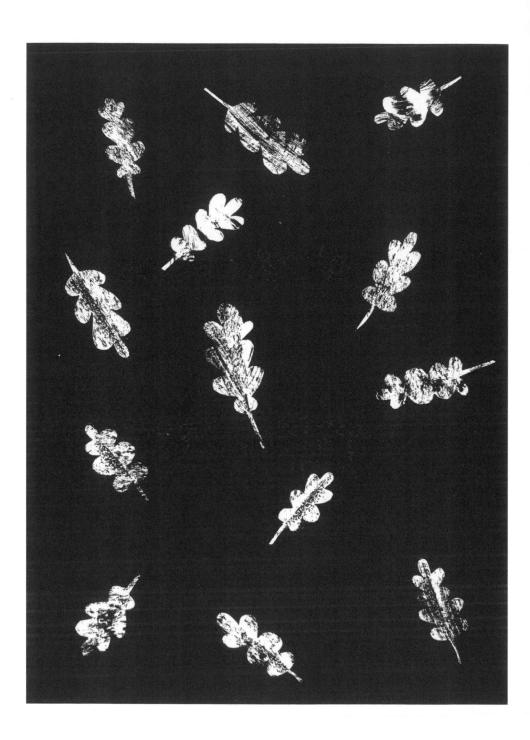

Marly Youmans is the author of three poetry collections, five novels, and several books of Southern fantasy for children. She is the winner of various national awards, including The Michael Shaara Award and The Ferrol Sams Award.

Currently she is serving on the judging panel for the 2012 National Book Award in Young People's Literature. Her 2012 books include the novel, *A Death at the White Camellia Orphanage* (Mercer University Press), and a collection of poems from Stanza Press (U.K.), *The Foliate Head*, featuring a cover and interior art by Clive Hicks-Jenkins.

A native of South Carolina, she grew up in Louisiana, North Carolina, and elsewhere. Ms. Youmans lives in the village of Cooperstown, New York with her husband and three children.

Clive Hicks-Jenkins has been called by Simon Callow "one of the most individual and complete artists of our time." His work is held in all the principal public collections in Wales and his artist's books with the Old Stile Press are in libraries worldwide. He exhibits regularly with the Martin Tinney Gallery in Cardiff.

His sixtieth-birthday retrospective exhibition at the National Library of Wales in 2011 was accompanied by two publications. The first was an anthology of 27 poems by American and British poets, *The Book of Ystwyth: Six Poets on the Art of Clive Hicks-Jenkins* (Carolina Wren Press), featuring Dave Bonta, Callum James, Andrea Selch, Catriona Urquhart, Damian Walford Davies and Marly Youmans. The second was a major study, *Clive Hicks-Jenkins* (Lund Humphries), with essays by, among others, Simon Callow, Kathe Koja and Marly Youmans.

His work may be seen at www.hicks-jenkins.com

ABOUT PHOENICIA PUBLISHING

Phoenicia Publishing is an independent press based in Montreal but involved, through a network of online connections, with writers and artists all over the world. We are interested in words and images that illuminate culture, spirit, and the human experience. A particular focus is on writing and art about travel between cultures—whether literally, through lives of refugees, immigrants, and travelers, or more metaphorically and philosophically—with the goal of enlarging our understanding of one another through universal and particular experiences of change, displacement, disconnection, assimilation, sorrow, gratitude, longing and hope.

We are committed to the innovative use of the web and digital technology in all aspects of publishing and distribution, and to making high-quality works available that might not be viable for larger publishers. We work closely with our authors, and are pleased to be able to offer them a greater share of royalties than is normally possible.

Your support of this endeavor is greatly appreciated.

Our complete catalogue is online at www.phoeniciapublishing.com

Made in the USA
Lexington, KY
14 June 2013